INSIDE THE MINDS

Litigation Strategies for Government Contracts

Leading Lawyers on Understanding the False Claims Act, Filing Bid Protests, and Working with Government Agencies

2015 EDITION

ASPATORE

For additional copies or customer service inquiries, please e-mail west.customer.service@thomson.com.

ISBN 978-0-314-29316-9

Mat #41715122

Praise for *Inside the Minds*

"This series provides a practical and focused discussion of the leading issues in law today." – John V. Biernacki, Partner, Jones Day

"*Inside the Minds* draws from the collective experience of the best professionals. The books are informative from an academic, and, more importantly, practical perspective. I highly recommend them." – Keith M. Aurzada, Partner, Bryan Cave LLP

"Aspatore's *Inside the Minds* series provides practical, cutting edge advice from those with insight into the real world challenges that confront businesses in the global economy." – Michael Bednarek, Partner, Shearman & Sterling LLP

"What to read when you want to be in the know—topical, current, practical, and useful information on areas of the law that everyone is talking about." – Erika L. Morabito, Partner, Patton Boggs LLP

"Some of the best insight around from sources in the know" – Donald R. Kirk, Shareholder, Fowler White Boggs PA

"The *Inside the Minds* series provides a unique window into the strategic thinking of key players in business and law." – John M. Sylvester, Partner, K&L Gates LLP

"Comprehensive analysis and strategies you won't find anywhere else." – Stephen C. Stapleton, Of Counsel, Dykema Gossett PLLC

"The *Inside the Minds* series is a real hands-on, practical resource for cutting edge issues." – Trey Monsour, Partner, Haynes and Boone LLP

"A tremendous resource, amalgamating commentary from leading professionals that is presented in a concise, easy to read format." – Alan H. Aronson, Shareholder, Akerman Senterfitt

"Unique and invaluable opportunity to gain insight into the minds of experienced professionals." – Jura C. Zibas, Partner, Lewis Brisbois Bisgaard & Smith LLP

"A refreshing collection of strategic insights, not dreary commonplaces, from some of the best of the profession." – Roger J. Magnuson, Partner, Dorsey & Whitney LLP

"Provides valuable insights by experienced practitioners into practical and theoretical developments in today's ever-changing legal world." – Elizabeth Gray, Partner, Willkie, Farr & Gallagher LLP

"This series provides invaluable insight into the practical experiences of lawyers in the trenches." – Thomas H. Christopher, Partner, Kilpatrick Stockton LLP

ASPATORE

Aspatore Books, a Thomson Reuters business, exclusively publishes C-Level executives and partners from the world's most respected companies and law firms. Each publication provides professionals of all levels with proven business and legal intelligence from industry insiders—direct and unfiltered insight from those who know it best. Aspatore Books is committed to publishing an innovative line of business and legal titles that lay forth principles and offer insights that can have a direct financial impact on the reader's business objectives.

Each chapter in the *Inside the Minds* series offers thought leadership and expert analysis on an industry, profession, or topic, providing a future-oriented perspective and proven strategies for success. Each author has been selected based on their experience and C-Level standing within the business and legal communities. *Inside the Minds* was conceived to give a first-hand look into the leading minds of top business executives and lawyers worldwide, presenting an unprecedented collection of views on various industries and professions.

CONTENTS

Government Contracts Litigation in 2014 and Beyond: More Protests and Enforcement Actions, Fewer but Better Claims, and ADR Early and Often

Aaron P. Silberman

Shareholder

Rogers Joseph O'Donnell PC

ASPATORE

Introduction

Recent trends in government contracts litigation have continued in 2014. Increased numbers of bid protests have persisted; enforcement actions are on the rise; and contract claims are on the decline. Substantive issues that have been brewing for years, such as cyber-security, counterfeit parts, foreign corrupt practices, and false claims against state and local governments, are coming to the fore, with more litigation activity and higher stakes for contractors than ever. Shrinking government dollars have led to fewer procurements, with varying impacts of disputes.

These developments put a premium on litigators for government contractors' doing their homework early. They should develop a deep understanding of all contract requirements—express, incorporated, or implied—and how they will likely be interpreted by the relevant fora for disputes. They should advise and help their clients investigate potential claims and liabilities thoroughly and in a timely manner. Government contracts litigators should also craft their litigation strategies to the type of contract, evaluate and advise their clients on alternatives to litigation early and throughout any dispute or litigation, and, wherever possible, work with government counsel toward a mutually beneficial resolution.

Recent Developments in Government Contracts and Litigation Strategies

Over the past several years, there has been an increase in bid protests, especially at the federal level and especially on information technology (IT) procurements. The Government Accountability Office (GAO), for example, saw dramatic increases in protest filings in 2009 and 2010 and has seen levels remain near these higher levels each year since.

This increase has also been noticeable on state-level IT, as well, and to a lesser degree on other state- and local-level procurements. This trend appears to be slowing in 2014, and exploration of more effective use of alternative dispute resolution (ADR), while in its nascent stages at the federal level and virtually unheard of at state and local levels, will likely have a significant impact in further reducing the frequency and duration of protests.

There has also been an increase in federal enforcement-type actions, such as those brought by the US Department of Justice (DOJ) and whistleblowers under the False Claims Act (FCA) and the DOJ under statutes such as the Anti-Kickback Act of 1986 and Foreign Corrupt Practices Act (FCPA), among many others. To the extent that states and local jurisdictions have similar laws, most notably false claims laws, they have witnessed similar increases, including increases in multidistrict litigations (MDLs) involving alleged false claims in many different jurisdictions. This trend has shown no indication of slowing in 2014; to the contrary, in at least some areas, such as the FCPA and state FCAs, this trend may be accelerating.

There has been a decrease in litigated contract claims over the past several years—for example, federal Contracts Disputes Act of 1978 (CDA) litigation before the federal Boards of Contract Appeals (BCAs) and the Court of Federal Claims (COFC). For federal claims, this may in large part be ascribed to a large increase in the use and effectiveness of ADR in Board of Contract Appeals and Court of Federal Claims matters. This may also be attributed in part to increased compliance and business system requirements for federal contractors, which, in many cases, may prevent disputes or at least limit their dollar values and so permit their resolution more often prior to or at the earliest stages of litigation. To the extent that contractors handle both federal and state/local procurement work, these same systems will have similar effects on their state and local business. For all of these reasons, this trend has continued in 2014 and is likely to continue in the near future.

Overall, with more battles being fought over solicitations and awards (in bid protests), greater enforcement litigation, and less claims litigation, contract scope is likely to be better defined from the outset (offset to a degree by ever-reducing numbers of qualified government procurement professionals); contractor compliance is likely to be more effective during performance; and claims are likely to be better documented and presented in a more timely manner to government agencies. In those increasingly rare cases in which a contractor has a large claim, one or all of these improvements will have broken down, and it will be litigation as usual. But, more often, the aforementioned improvements will narrow the issues and, where disputes persist, result in more streamlined litigation with less discovery needed (or, for protests, less need or justification for attempting to go beyond the administrative record), fewer material facts disputed, and so more effective dispositive motion practice and fewer trials, and an overall shorter time to resolution. Countering these somewhat are courts' and administrative tribunals' dwindling resources, which stretch out litigation schedules and increase litigation costs.

New Statutes, Regulations, and Rules

At the federal level, the buzzwords are "cyber-security" and "counterfeit parts." The rules for both are still developing, but these will clearly be sources of much government contract litigation in the years to come, starting as early as this year on some issues. Federal contractors will be required to adopt complicated and often vague federal cyber-security requirements. Some contractors will almost certainly not have adequate systems in place and will fail to comply, and some of those contractors will experience cyber-security breaches as a result. That is when the fireworks will start. Meanwhile, counterfeiting of electronics parts is a worldwide problem. As the federal government pushes down to its contractors (and their subcontractors and suppliers) the risks and responsibilities of counterfeit parts, compliance will become more difficult, breaches more common, and litigation more prevalent. This is especially so in the less-defined areas of the federal rules, such as treatment of legacy parts like spares.

While there have been no amendments to the federal FCA in 2014, court decisions promise to have an impact on FCA litigation this year and for many to come. A hot area has been contractor defenses, with more circuit court decisions coming out (and in some instances, Supreme Court decisions looming) on the statute of limitations, Rule 9(b) pleading particularity requirement, first-to-file bar, public disclosure bar, implied certification, and other issues. On balance, these decisions have probably favored contractors slightly, but this does not appear to have slowed the heavy trend toward greater government enforcement and whistleblower activity.

At the state level, there have been many legislative changes broadening state FCAs, most of which have taken effect in the last year. These have, by and large, been motivated and shaped by the federal Department of Health and

Human Services' enforcement of the federal Deficit Reduction Act of 2005, tying states' entitlements to a greater share of any recovered Medicaid funds to those states' maintaining FCAs "at least as effective in rewarding and facilitating qui tam actions" and their federal counterpart. Changes in various states to their FCAs have included:

1. Eliminating a requirement that a claim was presented to the government
2. Increasing civil penalties and making them available for all violations, rather than just for direct false claims, for calculating civil penalties
3. Increasing anti-retaliation protections
4. Lengthening statutes of limitations
5. Increasing government ability to object to dismissals on public disclosure grounds and a narrowed public disclosure defense
6. Allowing government employees to file actions without exhausting internal procedures
7. Authorizing courts to reduce shares of relators who planned and initiated violations

These have not only incentivized increased enforcement by state authorities and whistleblowers, but also increased contractor exposure. While the impact on the number and scope of state FCA litigations has not yet been quantified, these changes have almost certainly increased complaint filings in 2014 and beyond and will lead to increased recoveries, through both settlements and judgments. In the longer term, they will likely lead to greater contract compliance efforts by state government contractors, including business systems already familiar to federal contractors.

Investigating the Claim and Developing a Litigation Strategy

Knowledge of Government Contract Components

Contractors first need to understand the totality of requirements in their contracts. Government contracts are notoriously complex, often incorporating many documents by reference. At the federal level, such incorporated documents typically include the Federal Acquisition Regulation (FAR) and agency standard clauses and specifications. At the state and, less often, local levels, contracts may incorporate standard terms and conditions, general and specific to the type of contract. At all levels, the solicitation and proposal documents may be incorporated, in whole or in part. Government contracts are also often subject to many amendments. Clients, of course, should read and understand all such incorporated documents at contracting and amendments when made, but, in the all-too-common instances where they did not, and now a dispute is looming, understanding the entire contract is an important early step.

At the federal level, contractors also must take into account the Christian Doctrine, which will imply into federal contracts clauses that were omitted from the contract documents but were required by regulation and express "a significant or deeply ingrained strand of public procurement policy." Determining whether any omitted provisions will be implied under this doctrine first requires a review of what was included in the contract and identifying certain important contract characteristics, such as contract type (fixed price or cost reimbursement?), what is being procured (goods or services?), dollar value, commerciality, applicability of small or disadvantaged business programs, performance location (overseas?), and others. This may be a very difficult task. After required but omitted clauses are identified, the contractor must determine whether those clauses are significant enough to qualify for application of the Christian Doctrine, which will require reference to court and board decisions.

Once the contractor understands the totality of the contract requirements, it needs to evaluate whether there are any relevant conflicts among them and, if so, how they would likely be resolved by a relevant court or board. The first step is identifying all potentially relevant conflicts. Next, the contractor should look for an order of precedence clause or similar language; this is required in many federal government contracts and is quite common is government contracts at all levels. Then, the contractor must evaluate the applicable law on contract interpretation and resolution of internal contract conflicts. An important detail here is often whether the conflicting contract provisions were required by regulation (on federal contracts, the FAR and department/agency regulations) or, if not, whether they were boilerplate or otherwise imposed by the agency, or were negotiated by the parties or were suggested by the contractor. Finally, the contractor should research the relevant decisions of potential litigation venues.

A category of contract requirements that is often quite challenging, even to experienced government contractors, is subcontractor and supplier requirements. Contractors will often find it difficult to evaluate, and therefore comply with, these requirements. A persistent and often tricky question is whether a contract requirement must, may, or may not be flowed down. Some required federal contract clauses are mandatory flow downs, meaning the prime contractor is obligated under the prime contract to include the clause in its subcontracts and, in some cases, the subcontractors are required to flow the clauses further down the tiers, as well. Other clauses permit flow downs, while yet others prohibit them. Determining which type of flow down applies in turn will depend on many factors beyond simply the language of the prime contract requirement itself, such as the value of the subcontract and whether the subcontract is for a commercial item.

Where disputes over subcontract/supplier requirements end up in litigation, there are both legal and practical considerations. For contractor claims on federal contracts, the Severin Doctrine is a concern, albeit one that has been significantly watered down by court decisions over the past few decades. That doctrine does not allow a prime contractor to recover on a claim it sponsors for a subcontractor (a.k.a. a pass-through claim) if the prime contractor has no potential liability to the subcontractor for the claim. Careful contractors will overcome this hurdle by including in their subcontracts, or in subsequent pass-through claims agreements (a.k.a. liquidating agreements) provisions reserving the prime contractor's and subcontractor's respective rights against one another.

Prime contractors still face other, practical hurdles in litigating pass-through claims against a government agency, as well. The subcontractor may have claims against the prime contractor—for example, based on the latter's failure to provide timely notice to the government. The prime contractor and subcontractor, though teaming on this contract, may be competitors on other procurements, such that they do not want to share sensitive proprietary information that is relevant to the claim (and discoverable). The government may, based on a lack of contractual privity, refuse to deal directly with the subcontractor, even for purposes of negotiating a settlement. (This is especially a problem in pre-litigation attempts to settle a dispute.)

Determining Claim Legitimacy

Ideally, contractors will have systems in place—e.g., accounting, scheduling, and documentation—from the very start of every contract in order to track progress, time, and costs against the original scope of work, including character of that work, material and labor quantities, and planned schedule. This will ensure that determining and supporting a claim is already part of the contractor's performance process. Alas, litigation counsel do not live an ideal world.

It is absolutely essential that before a contractor submits a claim to a government agency, the contractor takes all reasonable steps, taking industry standard practices into account, to validate and document every element of that claim. Some contractors, particularly large, sophisticated ones that do a significant amount of government work, have many systems and resources in place to assist in this effort. Others—often smaller contractors or those who are primarily commercial providers—do not have such systems or resources and will have to invest in outside expertise, including outside counsel.

Outside counsel may be helpful in this due diligence process in at least two ways. First, there is always the possibility that potential contractor liabilities may emerge in investigating a contractor's affirmative claim. For example, the contractor may discover it was overpaid, submitted false claims, provided defective pricing to the government, or otherwise breached contract or other legal requirements. Having counsel lead the investigation, with proper measures taken to ensure confidentiality, will allow the contractor to protect the work product of the investigation under the attorney-client privilege and work product doctrine. This was the subject of an important recent FCA decision out of the D.C. Circuit, *In re Kellogg Brown & Root Inc.* While a contractor may accomplish the same benefit with in-house counsel, such counsel often has a dual, business/legal role, which may jeopardize the contractor's ability to maintain the privilege over certain material.

Second, outside counsel will, in many cases, be best suited to take a broad view, evaluating how to conduct the investigation based on the experiences of many different companies, using outside consultants in many different disciplines—e.g., in government cost accounting, engineering, business processes and government contracting industry practices, and labor productivity—and with an eye toward the possibility of litigation.

The last point is important because strategic issues in an investigation can, and likely will, affect a contractor's ability to succeed if its claim goes to litigation. For example, outside counsel can help the contractor decide strategically to conduct certain portions of the investigation outside the privilege, so that the work product of those portions may be disclosed to the government without waiving the privilege as to other efforts. Counsel may help the contractor decide which consultants it will plan to use only internally (such that their work product will not be discoverable in subsequent litigation) and which it will plan to disclose as testifying experts (such that everything they rely on is discoverable, and thus the information provided to them must be selected with greater care).

Litigation Strategies by Contract Type

Breach issues are generally the same regardless of contract type, with the primary exception being cases in which an alleged breach concerns cost-accounting obligations under cost-based contracts, such as cost reimbursement contracts. These most often are alleged contractor breaches, such as failure to keep adequate records, cooperate with government audits, and update the government on changes to contractors' costs and/or accounting systems. Although less common, alleged government breaches of such contracts arise, as well, such as excessive audits and failure to review and approve contractor systems or disclosures in a timely manner. These kinds of issues are much less common in disputes involving non-cost-based contracts, such as firm fixed price (FFP) contracts. Not surprisingly, hybrid contract types, such as cost-plus-fixed-fee contracts, lie somewhere in between.

Where cost- and non-cost-based contracts litigation most significantly differ is in calculating and proving damages. While litigating cost-based contract claims often requires more significant cost-accounting work and expertise than doing so for non-cost-based contract claims, it is often more necessary to get early and extensive outside consulting assistance to support damages claims for *non*-cost-based contracts. This is because contractors that do primarily cost-based government contracting by necessity have in-house systems and expertise to track and document their costs. This will give those contractors a huge head start on putting together their claims and will offer their litigation counsel ready-made resources, both as internal consultants and as testifying witnesses. To be sure, there is still a significant role to be played by outside consultants in cost-based contract claims litigation, to provide both the increased bandwidth litigation requires and the more objective, and therefore more credible, view of an outside party.

A crossover area in regard to cost- and non-cost-based contracts litigation is disputes over terminations for convenience (T4Cs) of FFP contracts. Under all FFP procurement contracts with the federal government, and under most with state and local governments, as well, the contractor recovery under a T4C is its costs incurred for work performed, plus a reasonable profit (or loss) on those costs, plus termination expenses. Thus, a T4C effectively converts an FFP contract into a cost-plus contract.

Where the parties dispute, and so litigate, the contractor's costs and reasonable profit or loss, the litigation issues more closely mirror those in a cost-based contract claim than those in an FFP contract claim, but there are some important differences. Most notably, since the terminated contract itself is not cost-based, it generally would not have required the contractor to have maintained nearly the same degree of cost records as would one under a cost-based contract. An outside cost-accounting expert will be needed earlier and more extensively to assist both on cost calculation and documentation and on reasonable profit or loss. Often, the litigating contractor will also be well served by an industry expert who can credibly consult and testify regarding the standard practices in the industry in areas such as cost tracking and documentation, subcontract and supply chain management, cost estimating at bidding, and reasonable profit, among others.

Alternatives to Litigation

There are several different, interrelated alternatives to litigating government contract disputes: dispute avoidance, escalation, and ADR. The extent to which these alternatives will be available and, if so, effective, depends largely on the agency, the contract, and applicable law and regulation. All of them, where effectively used, promise a combination of the same benefits as compared with litigation:

- Better contract performance—e.g., better quality, shorter delivery time, lower costs
- More efficient and effective conflict resolution—e.g., faster resolution, better project and long-term/relationship outcomes for all parties
- Better ability to anticipate and manage risk

Dispute avoidance is typically built into the contract, either initially or by amendment. It is designed to manage the parties' interactions so that issues that arise during performance are resolved before they significantly impact the work and fester into larger disputes. Two examples, seen most frequently on large government construction contracts, are project neutrals and dispute review boards (DRBs). Both methods involve appointing an independent person or persons to monitor contract performance and provide guidance on resolution of issues, ranging from contract interpretation (e.g., determining whether work is in or out of scope) to scheduling (e.g., quantifying and assigning responsibility for a delay) to engineering (e.g., reconciling conflicting project design documents) to cost (e.g., quantifying cost impacts of delays, disruptions, and extra work).

For all but the smallest and simplest contracts, dispute avoidance, on some scale, is often a cost-effective way of improving contract results. As the success of dispute avoidance clauses gains wider recognition, their use will likely increase, not just on government construction projects, but also in government contracts across industries. Those with complicated performance issues, such as large weapons systems and IT contracts, are particularly good candidates for adoption of this method.

Escalation is essentially informal, party-to-party ADR. It may also be called formalized common sense. Like dispute avoidance, escalation is typically built into the contract. An escalation clause will require the parties to take one or more steps to try to resolve disputes as prerequisites to more formal, substantial actions, such as filing a lawsuit or initiating formal ADR. The most effective escalation will require, at least as one of its steps, that the parties raise a dispute to executives above the project level. This helps get issues before individuals without personal stakes (or at least with much more diminished personal stakes) in a project. A government contracting officer or contractor project manager may have difficulty ignoring the impact of a contract claim on his or her job performance evaluation and so may be less able to come to a sensible resolution in both parties' interest. A government division or department director or a contractor regional or business sector executive may not face the same impediments. Escalation clauses are not required under federal regulation, but they are not precluded, either. They are common in commercial contracts and are appearing more and more in government contracts at all levels.

Last but not least, formal ADR remains the predominant alternative to litigation of government contract disputes, and its use continues to grow. The primary forms of ADR for government contracts are arbitration and mediation. Arbitration, with appropriate constraints (e.g., on discovery, motion practice, and appeal rights), may be less costly and will almost always take less time than court litigation. Its greatest advantage may be the ability of the parties to select an arbitrator, or panel, with subject matter expertise, something the parties often cannot find in a court judge, much less a jury. This is especially an advantage for state and local government contracts, though still an advantage for federal government contracts as well, despite the availability of specialized fora for protests and claims—i.e., the GAO, COFC, BCAs, and Federal Circuit. Government regulation and policy, as well as underlying concerns about issues such as transparency and the vibrancy of court precedents, sometimes deter government use of arbitration.

On the other hand, governments at all levels increasingly are embracing mediation as a way to avoid litigation. This ADR method suffers from many of the same impediments contractors face in efforts to settle disputes with government agencies generally. Agencies are often limited in their authority, or at least willingness, to settle disputes broadly—for example, to resolve both civil and criminal liability, debarment, and extra-contractual liability, such as that under false claims laws. Still, despite these impediments, mediation is generally a highly effective method for resolving most government contract disputes. At the federal level, the government has already recognized this for contract claims and is exploring use of mediation in bid protests.

Working with Government Agencies during the Litigation Process

There is no better method for working with the government agency during the litigation process than for you, as contractor's counsel, to develop open lines of communication with agency counsel and, to the maximum extent possible, to engender that counsel's trust. This starts long before the litigation of any particular case or the representation of any particular client.

Making thoughtful, balanced contributions to the government contracting community—and, more specifically, the government contracts bar—legitimizes you as more than just a "hired gun." It also allows you to make personal connections with inside counsel for agencies and the DOJ and state and local equivalents. Those connections additionally allow you, as contractor's counsel, both to develop and to demonstrate your understanding of the government's issues and interests. If you then litigate a particular dispute with a particular agency, you may have personal contacts with the government counsel assigned to the dispute or peers of that counsel within the same agency, and, even when those personal contacts do not exist, as contractor counsel, you will find it invaluable to have a reputation as a straight shooter who generally understands the government's perspective on contract issues.

Once you are engaged by a contractor in connection with a dispute, you should look for the earliest opportunity—always, of course, keeping your client's interests in mind—to reach out to government counsel to start a dialog about the dispute and how best to resolve it. Where settlement negotiation or ADR are potentially beneficial, as they often are, these should be early subjects of discussion. But even where the client is resolved to litigate vigorously, developing a professional working relationship with government counsel still almost always serves your client's best interests.

You can often start this relationship on the right foot by attempting to find common ground on issues that need not be adversarial, such as litigation scheduling, preferred methods of service, and early exchange of relevant, discoverable, and available documents. Other issues may also be helpful to discuss before any rules require it, such as electronic documents and discovery and witness identification and interviews. Rather than taking advantage of stretched government attorney resources, you should consider instances in which your own client's interests will be served by making the government counsel's job easier, thereby avoiding needless and petty disputes that cost both clients' time and money. Coming full circle, even in the most contentious of litigations, you should always keep an eye out for ADR and settlement opportunities and counsel your client when they appear.

Effect of Increased Competition for Fewer Government Contracts

The impact of a decreasing number of contract competitions will depend largely on whether opportunities in the private sector are also decreasing or, instead, are staying the same or increasing. Where private sector opportunities are increasing in an industry, the decline in government business will not significantly affect the relative number of protests. Many contractors will simply go elsewhere—i.e., put more resources into getting private sector work. This dynamic does not apply, however, in those industries for which business is exclusively, or almost exclusively, government business. And, even in industries that service both government and private sectors, if the private sector opportunities dry up as quickly as or faster than those for government work, then protests will increase as government competitions decrease—contractors are left to fight for the scraps.

Where protests increase in part because of a decrease in private sector opportunities, there will often be an increase in new entrants to government contract competitions. This puts a premium on an agency's duty to communicate its requirements clearly and to evaluate bidder responsibility. These duties are intertwined because agencies are often vague in solicitations about responsibility requirements—i.e., what financial resources, prior experience, references, etc., a bidder must have in order fall within the agency's tolerance for risk on a project. New entrants to government contracting are often vulnerable to failure to meet the agency's actual responsibility requirements. Yet, if a solicitation ill-defines these requirements, this—combined with fiscal pressures to accept the lowest-priced proposal and the legal difficulties in justifying rejection of a proposal for bidder non-responsibility—often renders agencies unable, or at least unwilling, to exercise their right to reject on this basis.

Theoretically, a decrease in the number of competitions should result in higher-quality procurements by mitigating a persistent problem in government contracting: the significant lack of experienced, qualified contracting professionals within government. Given more available resources to evaluate potential procurements, develop specifications, prepare solicitations, evaluate proposals, and make awards, agencies should tend to do a better job complying with the law and getting the best value of the taxpayer. Unfortunately, the government's ability to realize these benefits is hampered by the inevitable diversion of resources in a slowdown from procurement to other functions. Nevertheless, one legal impact of a decrease in competitions on protests is that, because of a margin improvement in procurements, there will be a corresponding decrease in the proportion of protests that are taken well.

Finally, a significant issue arising from a decrease in the number of competitions is its effect in combination with the concurrent dramatic increase in the cost of preparing and submitting proposals for government work. As agencies have bundled more and increasingly complex requirements, the financial investment of bidding on government contracts has risen and will continue to do so. A serious concern arising from these trends is whether the reduction in competitions will have a disparate impact on small- and medium-sized businesses. Small business programs lessen this impact for some, but exclude the many others that cannot afford to bid in general competitions and are not eligible for small business preferences or set-asides. Counsel for such clients can best assist their clients by raising these issues as early as possible with the contracting agencies, ideally before a solicitation is even issued—e.g., where the agency issues a request for information (RFI) or otherwise does market research, where it advertises an upcoming opportunity, or the client otherwise knows of such an opportunity—or, at the very least, before bid submission—e.g., through bidder conferences or questions or, where permitted, in a pre-award requirements protest.

Conclusion

Recent changes in litigating government contracts have mostly been further extensions of existing trends. While some of the substantive requirements being litigated are new (like cyber-security and counterfeit parts) or getting increased attention (like the FCPA and state false claims laws), the procedural and strategic issues in litigation are variations on familiar themes: more protests, greater enforcement, fewer claims, and more ADR.

Overall spending has gone down at all levels of government and is likely to continue to do so in the near term, resulting in fewer procurements to protest and fewer contracts to dispute. The impact of this reduction on litigation will depend on a myriad of other factors, such as the commercial economy and the extent to which governments further reduce their procurement staffs. In the end, litigators for government contractors will best serve their clients as they always have: by doing their homework and helping their clients understand all of their contract rights and obligations and by fighting with the government wherever necessary, but working with it wherever possible.

Key Takeaways

- Make sure your client reads government contracts carefully. Contractors first need to understand the totality of requirements in their contracts.
- Take into account the Christian Doctrine, which will imply into federal contracts clauses that were omitted from the contract documents but were required by regulation and express "a significant or deeply ingrained strand of public procurement policy."
- Evaluate the applicable law on contract interpretation and resolution of internal contract conflicts. Research the relevant decisions of potential litigation venues.
- Contractors must, before submitting a claim to a government agency, take all reasonable steps, taking industry standard practices in account, to validate and document every element of that claim.
- As a contractor's counsel, develop open lines of communication with agency counsel and, to the maximum extent possible, engender that counsel's trust. Making thoughtful, balanced contributions to the government contracting community and, more specifically, the government contracts bar, legitimizes you as more than just a "hired gun."

Aaron P. Silberman is a shareholder in the San Francisco office of Rogers Joseph O'Donnell PC, where he is a member of the firm's Construction and Government Contracts Practice Groups. Mr. Silberman has specialized in construction and public contracts advice and litigation since 1992. He has represented contractors, subcontractors, suppliers, and design professionals in the construction, defense, technology, telecom, and service industries. His experience includes contracts for federal, state, and local public entities. He has helped clients evaluate, negotiate, and draft solicitations, clarification questions, proposals, and bids; negotiated and evaluated proposed contract terms; litigated bid protests of public contract awards; investigated and litigated claims for delay, disruption, payment, defects, and fraud or false claims; and advised clients and litigated disputes in connection with contract terminations, suspension and debarment, bond requirements, payment issues, and disabled access issues.

Mr. Silberman has spoken and published articles on a wide variety of government contracts and construction law subjects, including false claims, terminations, bid protests, subcontracting, building information modeling (BIM), green building, Energy Savings Performance Contracts, information technology (IT) procurements, abandonment/ cardinal change claims, disabled access, and licensing.

A leader in several prominent government contracts and construction organizations, Mr. Silberman serves as an officer of the American Bar Association (ABA) Public Contract Law Section and is a former member of the Section Council and a past chair of its Federal Procurement, State & Local Procurement, and Construction Divisions and its Procurement Fraud and Strategic Alliances, Teaming and Subcontracting committees. He chairs the Publication Committee of the ABA Forum on the Construction Industry and is a past member of the Governing Committee and past chair of its Specialty Trade Contractors & Suppliers Division. He is the chair of the Board of Directors of the Bay Area District of Associated General Contractors (AGC)-California, is a former chair of the AGC-C's Legal Advisory Committee, and is a former member of its Executive Committee.

Education, Perseverance, and Patience: Necessary Components of Winning Government Contract Disputes

Michael L. Sterling

Managing Partner

Vandeventer Black LLP

ASPATORE

Introduction

Litigation starts long before an appeal is filed at an agency board or a case is filed in court. General knowledge of the government contract dispute process is a crucial foundation to a good litigation strategy. The dispute process is influenced by political decisions and the economy. Decisions by policy makers to change programs and by contractors to pursue new opportunities have altered the landscape of disputes. The growth of electronically stored information (ESI) has also had a profound impact on dispute resolution and litigation in all forums.

The comments in this chapter review recent trends and developments in government contracts that affect the dispute process and litigation. I have included references to notable cases and regulatory provisions that will help you develop a winning strategy.

Trends and Developments in Government Contracts

At the top of the list of recent developments in government contracts is the increasing focus on utilization of small business entities, whether veteran-, woman-, or minority-owned. While many programs have existed for a number of years, there seems to be a growing political and administrative emphasis to make use of such programs. This has had a ripple effect on many aspects of government contracting, including the dispute resolution process.

While the demand to utilize such programs grows, there is increasing concern that the businesses are actually small and otherwise qualified. When a dispute arises on a contract subject to such programs, whether between the federal government and the contractor or the prime contractor and a subcontractor, it is crucial to audit the contract for compliance before pursuing the dispute. Otherwise, you might open a Pandora's box of non-compliance issues that will emerge during resolution of the dispute.

Another developing area is more aggressive claims by the government for alleged defective or incomplete contract work. On fixed-priced contracts and time-and-material contracts, the government is bringing claims, in some cases, for work that was done many years in the past. The government appears to be looking for ways to recover revenue on those old contracts. To help protect against this risk, it is important for clients to re-examine their record retention policies. Contractors should be thinking about whether they are doing a proper job of retaining records that would allow them to defend against such claims.

A third important development concerns the enforceability of choice of forum clauses on government contracts. This subject is close to me because I was involved in bringing the most recent case on the issue to the United States Supreme Court.[1] As contractors hire subcontractors and vendors to perform government contract work in multiple jurisdictions, the enforceability of forum selection clauses is of great importance.

The next development relates to the growing awareness of the impact from the amendment to the False Claims Act (FCA)[2] by the Fraud Enforcement and Recovery Act of 2009 (FERA).[3] While the amendments to the FCA exposed contractors to increased liability, it has taken several years for the risk to influence whether contractors are willing to submit requests for equitable adjustment and claims. Contractors are more cautious and more willing to seek accounting and legal help. They are more worried about submitting something that is inadequate or false, fearing they may expose themselves to some very steep damages from the government.

A related issue is the effort by prime contractors to flow down requirements to lower-tier subcontractors and vendors. In the past, if a subcontractor or vendor presented a request for equitable adjustment or a claim to a prime contractor, there was a general high-level review by the prime contractor to assess whether it was in good faith. Now there is greater concern and more extensive review of lower-tier submissions.

An issue affecting all litigation is the growth of ESI. E-discovery has been the focus of the federal courts and now the boards of contract appeals. Lawyers must consider how the federal government retains ESI and how to

---

[1] *Atl. Marine Constr. Co. v. U.S. Dist. Ct. for the W. Dist. of Tex.*, 134 S. Ct. 568 (2013).
[2] False Claims Act, 31 U.S.C. §§ 3729–3733 (2012).
[3] Fraud Enforcement and Recovery Act of 2009, Pub. L. No. 111-21, 123 Stat. 1617 (codified as amended in scattered sections of 18 U.S.C. and 31 U.S.C.).

go through e-discovery. This is going to become an increasing area of concern in government contract disputes.

A final contract trend relating to litigation is the increasing use of alternative dispute resolution (ADR). There has always been a healthy use of ADR at the boards of contract appeals, but the federal courts are making increased use of ADR as opposed to simply requiring a settlement conference. I think that is a trend that will continue because of docket congestion and concerns about the cost of litigation. In addition, the government is using more multiple-award and task-order contracts, where the contractor's positive relationship with the government is more crucial. This is because the contractor must deal with the same government officials for additional work, so if the parties resolve an issue through ADR instead of a contentious dispute and litigation process, they can help preserve that relationship.

Other Recent Developments

Attorneys need to monitor problems at the US Department of Veterans Affairs (VA). The media have paid a great deal of attention to the way the VA has been running health care facilities, and the VA has also been at the top of the list of agencies that have serious problems with contracts. There is a well-established regime of small-business programs at the US Small Business Administration (SBA). Yet, instead of relying on those programs and simply adding a new category for servicing disabled veterans, the VA established its own VetBiz program. In some cases, the VetBiz program has serious inconsistencies and conflicts with the SBA regulations that have led to long delays in processing applications by small businesses owned by service-disabled veterans.

Another consideration is the effect of the economy. Increased competition for government contracts in the down economy has reduced profit margins. That is not necessarily very good for either the contractor or the government. Less qualified people end up doing the work, and companies struggle to survive. Aside from that pure economic consideration, there is greater risk of poor performance. With a declining market for work, contractors who have become accustomed to doing work for which they have developed expertise look for other markets. It drastically increases risk if a contractor has been doing work on contracts for one agency, but then then starts doing work for another agency. The new work may have more challenges than the contractors recognize.

To further complicate things, some contractors have even changed their services and products. Some may go to a different region or even overseas. There are many more small- to mid-sized contractors exploring international contracting opportunities, which previously were pursued only by large contractors. The risks involved in those contracts are distinctly different from the risks from domestic contracts.

Noteworthy Cases

One important case that I already mentioned is *Atlantic Marine Construction Co. v. United States District Court for the Western District of Texas*.[4] The key issue decided is which party has the burden of proof when a party seeks to enforce or avoid a forum selection clause in federal court. The court held that the party acting in violation of the forum selection clause has the burden of proof.[5] 28 U.S.C. § 1404[6] codified a doctrine that allowed cases to be transferred to a more convenient forum, rather than being dismissed.[7]

Because both Section 1404 and the *forum non conveniens* doctrine from which it derives depend on a balancing-of-interests standard, courts should use that standard when evaluating claims under Section 1404.[8] The court also held that when parties have agreed to a forum selection clause, a court should transfer the case to that forum unless there are exceptional factors at work.[9] Those factors do not include ones that the parties were able to consider when they entered into the agreement with the forum selection clause.[10] The court's ruling makes it very important for all parties to be aware of choice-of-forum issues. Such clauses will have a significant impact on litigation strategy and cost.

---

4 *Atl. Marine Constr. Co.*, 134 S. Ct. 568.
5 *Id.* at 581.
6 28 U.S.C. § 1404 (2012).
7 *Id.* at 580.
8 *Id.*
9 *Id.* at 582.
10 *Id.*

Another case of significance is *Metcalf Construction Company Inc. v. United States.*[11] The *Metcalf* decision addresses the scope of the government's duty of good faith and fair dealing. The court of appeals rejected a narrow reading of the duty and held that the duty limits government acts or omissions that are inconsistent with the contract's purpose and deprive the contractor of contemplated value.[12] Basically, the court ruled that the government is obligated to deal in good faith and fairly with contractors.[13] That case and the implied duty should be considered in connection with any dispute.

Another important recent case is *United States of America ex rel. Harry Barko v. Halliburton Co.*[14] The *Barko* decision addresses the limits of the attorney-client privilege and the work product doctrine to prevent disclosure of ethics investigation files during discovery. It is a very interesting and important decision that government contract attorneys should review, as it demonstrates the need to follow a careful procedure in an ethics investigation. According to the court, neither the attorney-client privilege nor the work product doctrine prevented disclosure.[15] The relator sought almost 100 documents related to internal audit and fraud investigations conducted by one of the contractors. The documents were reviewed by the court *in camera* and described them as "eye-openers." Investigation documents can be protected from disclosure only under certain circumstances. The court will consider several factors, including the existence of a written code of business conduct that is followed by the company, a request for legal advice, attorney oversight of the investigation, written instructions from the attorney to any investigators, *Upjohn*[16] warnings to all current and former employees explaining that the interviews are for the purpose of providing legal advice to the company, restrictive labels on documents, reports addressed to the attorney, and a documented threat of litigation. Every company should have a written code of business conduct, and investigations should be planned with care.

---

11 *Metcalf Constr. Co. Inc. v. United States*, 742 F.3d 984 (Fed Cir. 2014).
12 *Id.* at 991.
13 *See id.* at 993-94.
14 *United States ex rel. Barko v. Halliburton Co.*, No. 1:05-CV-1276, 2014 WL 1016784 (D.D.C. Mar. 6, 2014).
15 *Id.* at *3.
16 *See Upjohn Co. v. United Sates*, 449 U.S. 383 (1981).

Finally, I note an important decision from the Southern District of New York regarding ESI and the need for claimants to protect against spoliation.[17] One of the leading jurists on e-discovery issues, Judge Shira Scheindlin, ruled that not only potential defendants, but also potential plaintiffs have a duty to preserve evidence.[18] This includes the requirement to suspend routine document destruction practices under an existing retention plan.

Subjects of Contract Disputes

Disputes are always about money. The biggest problem is whether the contractor should be paid more or the government should get money back. That is usually the underlying issue, but what leads to the dispute varies.

The type of contract, however, may be an important factor in whether a dispute develops and whether it leads to litigation. For many years, the federal government used primarily fixed-price contracts where substantial risk was placed on the contractor, but the government bore the risk that it wrote a proper requirement. The contractor could request a change order, submit a request for equitable adjustment, or pursue a claim.

The government has shifted toward using other types of contracts. For example, on construction projects, more design-build versus design-bid-build contracts are used. The contractor does more of the drafting of the requirement and therefore assumes more of the risk. It is then harder to pursue a claim. The case law addressing these shifts in responsibility is still developing.

Another issue is what I will call "subtle regulations and requirements." Some things are apparent on the face of every contract, but there are other things that are incorporated by reference. With every passing year, it seems that more regulations and requirements are incorporated by reference. This means there are more opportunities for contractors to miss items and have a dispute over whether something was properly incorporated and whether a change or equitable adjustment is required.

---

[17] *Sekisui Am. Corp. v. Hart*, 945 F. Supp. 2d 494 (S.D.N.Y. 2013).
[18] *See id.* at 507.

Government Contract Components

Before bidding on a contract, everyone should read it. This sounds elementary, but it is critically important for contractors to read their contracts, and not just the faces of the documents. Understanding the underlying legal obligations that are in rules and regulations is terribly important. That rolls forward into deciding whether a change order is appropriate and whether a request for equitable adjustment or claim should be submitted. Often, these initial steps are done without legal counsel's involvement. Many times, cases come to the lawyer's desk in their maturity after a notice was or was not submitted on time or after a request for equitable adjustment or a claim was submitted. If contractors have not thought through all of the requirements, they can create a hopeless situation. There is no limit on how much knowledge contractors should have about the legal regime in the area where they are doing business.

Among the most important provisions in contracts are the notice provisions. They may show up on the face of the contract or in a clause that is incorporated by reference. This is an important issue on federal, state, and local contracts. At the federal level, there are some equitable opportunities to overcome deficient notices, but they often do not exist at the state and local levels.

Another important clause is the statement of work. Often, contractors bid job B thinking that it is the same as job A, but they have not read the statement carefully enough to realize there are subtle differences. That can result in catastrophe. It is important to appreciate fully the scope of work applicable to the contract. Tied to that, contractors must see whether there have been any changes in the legal developments since they did the prior, seemingly similar, work.

Preparing for Litigation

Determining the Strength of Claims

Determining the strength of a claim requires several steps. One step is to direct the contractor initially to do its own information gathering to make sure it has the contract documents and basic information on what occurred.

It is typically good to have the contract team generate this information. Depending on the size of the contract, that could be one person or a half-dozen people who help put the information together initially. If the company presents that information in an organized format, it is more efficient and effective for legal review. Then, the attorney can ask follow-up questions, dig more deeply, and peel the onion back further to get additional information, rather than just sorting through everything from scratch.

The next step is to meet with the client and review the issue. Often, the people responsible for obtaining awards or running a project lose sight of the fact that they made a mistake, and it may not be a government problem. Therefore, it is prudent to seek input from company personnel who understand the issue, but who were not directly involved.

A third step is to determine whether to get advice from other professionals, such as accountants, engineers, scheduling analysts, or anyone else who can help analyze the details concerning the issue to determine whether it has potential merit. Experts can contribute at different levels, depending on the circumstance. For example, there might be an issue about a technical requirement. An independent expert might review that and opine as to whether there is likely an error on the government's part or whether it is something the contractor did not understand. It could be a financial issue, determining whether an adjustment is due or whether the amount proposed by the contractor or by the government is correct.

Supporting Clients New to Litigating Contracts with the Federal Government

Education is the key issue. Make sure the client understands how the process works: what needs to be done to pursue the process, the estimated cost, and then the buy-in. A company is not served well if it starts a process and abandons it because the company did not understand it or was not prepared to devote the necessary resources.

One of the costs that do not receive as much focus as they ought is the human workforce. Often, a client will ask for a litigation budget, then an expert budget, but will not ask the third question about the hours its own staff will need to put in. It is also important for lawyers to consider that during a lengthy claims process, the client's staff will likely be reassigned. The cost of the staffing needed to pursue a dispute is something that always must be taken into account by the client.

Collecting Information

Start with basic contract documents specifications, drawings applicable to the project statement of work, and then the particular regulations that apply. Some agencies have sub-regulations that are often overlooked, and they need to be dug out.

Then, usually, it is good to build a timeline to see how the contract and dispute evolved. A good starting point for the timeline is key correspondence, which typically means e-mails. It is also important to review the financial information. For other information, you need to find out what form it is in, how it is kept, how it is stored, and how it could be sorted and analyzed.

While taking these steps, consider things like notice, and ensure that the proper steps have been taken in order to preserve a claim. Also, make sure that the information is being presented properly. The three words to focus on are how, when, and why.

An increasing amount of data is ESI, so it is a matter of being able to mine the ESI in an organized fashion. The old-fashioned way of opening a file drawer and looking at documents page-by-page is often not feasible. The amount of data created by daily e-mail traffic has created so many bytes of data that there needs to be an organized, efficient way to review that information for what is most likely to be helpful.

Developing a Strategy

Today, the biggest challenge in developing a strategy is coming up with an economically viable plan. The cost of every aspect of pursuing a claim or engaging in litigation has increased, but sometimes the amount in dispute has not increased commensurately. A big challenge is strategizing with the client to come up with a means to pursue the claim in a way that could be economically beneficial to the company.

Determining Suitable Return on Investment in the Dispute

Review the various financial results that could be achieved. Review the impact on the current contract, and consider the affect on future contracts. Help the client think through whether the investment in pursuing the dispute is going to be worth the return. There are some circumstances where clients should be motivated to spend a tremendous amount of time and effort over seemingly small amounts because of long-term ramifications. For example, there may be a fine for a safety violation that may not be warranted. That may be worth a very long, hard fight because having that on the company record could have significant negative consequences. Similarly, adverse past performance evaluations may have an adverse impact on future awards.

Steps That Differ from Those in Commercial Litigation

A key component of pursuing a government contract dispute that is different from the commercial context is the availability of information through the Freedom of Information Act (FOIA).[19] Take full advantage of FOIA.

Also, always be aware of regulatory provisions that address subpoenaing witnesses. There are often special requirements that must be followed before you can obtain the testimony of a government employee. Review these requirements carefully. They usually extend the period of time that it takes to obtain access to government witnesses. Always learn whether the particular contract may have top-secret or secret information for which you need clearance to view. Plan to make sure you have the right people involved in your litigation team to get access to that data.

Litigation Timeline

First, you need to make sure the client submits its notices on time. Those can be very short timelines: ten, twenty-one, or thirty days, depending on the circumstance, terms of the contract, and applicable regulations. Following notices, the change order proposal, request for equitable

[19] Freedom of Information Act, 5 U.S.C. § 552 (1966).

adjustment, or a claim must each be submitted in a timely manner. Then, the issue is pushing the government to give you a response and then deciding whether to appeal an adverse decision. Once you have a final decision, you need to file a timely appeal. The appeal timeline will vary depending on whether you proceed to an agency board or court.

Managing the Litigation Process

Many well-regarded software packages are available on the commercial market to manage documents, cases, depositions, and videos. There are myriad great products, and the product choice may be driven by the nature of the dispute. Some product choices may be geographically driven, based on what court reporter services offer. Some product choices are driven by what the agency uses or what clients want to use. It is important to evaluate what meets the clients' needs.

Best Practices for Working with Government Agencies

I am a firm believer that you can catch more flies with honey than with vinegar. Cooperate. It is generally not wise to be boisterous, angry, loud, or forceful. It is appropriate to be stern, to stand by your client, and to stand up for your client's rights, but that needs to be done appropriately and courteously.

I always keep in mind that there is a great shortage of contract administrators (whether a contracting officers or their representatives), and there is a shortage of government attorneys. They need time to do what they need to do, and often if you push too hard, you can get an answer of "no" simply because it is easy for them to say that quickly. If you work with them a little, you may get a "yes."

Improving Outcomes

An ounce of prevention is worth a pound of cure. I try to work with my clients in advance as much as possible to avoid litigation, but if litigation becomes inevitable, I make sure the client is prepared. Work with clients to make sure they have sound documents, reliable systems, a capable team of people, a solid understanding of the process, and competent recordkeeping. These steps drastically increase the opportunity for success.

Assuming you do not have the opportunity to work with a client early in the process, the next most important thing is to try to encourage clients to let you do your homework. Clients tend to be impatient. They come to you with a problem, and they want you to do something right away. Often, the best answer is to be patient. Do your homework; do it right; dig deeply. Make sure you know what you are saying, and get the facts right before moving forward.

Obstacles in Government Contract Litigation

Difficulty Locating Records and Witnesses

Some records and witnesses may be difficult to find. The contractor may seek legal advice many years after performing the work. The nature of government contracts may lead to work in remote places—either in the United States or in different parts of the world—which may pose similar challenges to finding the evidence. These are issues to review when you first consult with the client.

Declining Number of Qualified Personnel

Another big problem is the declining number of personnel able to handle complex contract actions. It is a huge problem, and one person can do only so much work in one day. As people retire, are let go, or are bought out from these government agencies, it is becoming more difficult for them to run their programs. On a program-by-program, agency-by-agency basis, budget declines may cancel or shrink a program, but at the same time, there is a shrinking staff of people government-wide to run these programs. This leads to many errors and often to disputes that could have been avoided and often the inability of personnel to explain actions.

Conclusion

Government contract disputes and litigation will continue, and there will always be changes to programs, regulations, and the landscape influenced by the economy. While it is important to monitor changes, the fundamental concepts remain the same: determine the how, when, and why the dispute arose; educate the client; persevere; be patient; and you will prevail with a winning strategy.

Key Takeaways

- Make sure that clients re-examine their record retention policies, thinking through how long in the future a dispute might arise.
- Before bidding on a contract, everyone should read it. Read and understand not just the face of the document, but what is incorporated by reference.
- When determining a suitable return on investment in the dispute, review the various financial results that could be achieved; review the impact on the current contract; and consider the impact on future contracts.
- When litigating government contracts, take full advantage of the Freedom of Information Act to obtain information.

Michael L. Sterling is the managing partner of Vandeventer Black LLP, as well as the former manager of the firm's Construction and Government Contract Department and the firm's Dispute Resolution Services. He is also a mediator and arbitrator for the American Arbitration Association. He has appeared before numerous agencies and courts on government contract matters.

Mr. Sterling earned his BA (cum laude) *in economics from Lawrence University and his JD (Order of the Coif & Order of the Barrister) from the College of William & Mary School of Law. He has been recognized in* Best Lawyers in America, *and he is peer-rated AV in Martindale-Hubble. He can be contacted at 757-446-8600 or msterling@vank.com.*

The *Franconia Associates* Line of "THAT WAS THE DEAL" Cases: A Roadmap for Suing Uncle Sam for Breach of Contract while Successfully Navigating the Rocky Shoals of Sovereignty, Unmistakability, and Other Unmentionables

Jeff H. Eckland

Partner

Eckland & Blando LLP

ASPATORE

Introduction

We are fortunate to live in a nation that cherishes, even if it may not necessarily celebrate, freedom of contract. Citizens respect the contractual rights of other citizens and generally satisfy their own contractual obligations. The success of our economy, most agree, depends upon the fulfillment of mutual contractual obligations. For this reason, the common law of contracts enforces such obligations. But what happens when the contracting party staring us down from the other side of the table is none other than Uncle Sam? What is different? What is the same?

Freedom of Contract

The first place one generally looks for answers to such questions is that wellspring of basic rights, the United States Constitution. Strangely enough, however, the US Constitution does not itself protect the sanctity of contracts between United States citizens and their federal government. Rather, the actual text of the US Constitution is altogether silent on the question of "government contracts." And the only language contained in the US Constitution that does address contracts requires only that no *state* shall pass any law impairing the obligation of contracts,[1] which contracts have been construed to include both commercial and government contracts.[2] Nor does the Bill of Rights—the fundamental progenitor of our individual freedoms—specifically enumerate freedom of contract as among our most precious rights. Indeed, the US Supreme Court has held that the privilege to sue the government for breach of contract is not a grant of a property right protected by the Fifth Amendment.[3] Thus, by silence if not by implication, the text of the US Constitution—although it does not condone breaches of contract by the federal government—certainly does not require Uncle Sam to reward US citizens with the benefit of their bargains.

---

[1] US CONST. art. I, § 10, cl. 6.

[2] "The Contracts Clause does not specifically refer to government contracts. ... Since *Fletcher v. Peck* in 1810, however, the Clause has been construed to restrict the power of the states to enact legislation impairing their own obligations under contract." Gillian Hadfield, *Of Sovereignty and Contract: Damages for Breach of Contract by Government*, 8 S. CAL. INTERDISC. L.J. 467, 480 (1999) (citing *Fletcher v. Peck*, 40 U.S. (6 Cranch) 87 (1810)).

[3] *Lynch v. United States*, 292 U.S. 571, 581-82 (1934).

Thus, the inviolability of contracts and the mutuality of obligations under them have never depended upon the dictates of the US Constitution, nor does the law of contracts spring from most constitutions or similar governing documents in other countries around the world. Nonetheless, legal protection has been afforded to contracts for hundreds of years on several continents. Such protection flows from the essence of that thing called the common law, the law handed down by courts—i.e., judge-made law to protect manmade rights.

Fortunately for US citizens, the federal common law of contracts appears alive and well. Each year, the US government contracts with private individuals, small businesses, corporations, and other legal entities for hundreds of billions of dollars' worth of goods and services. Many of these contracts are procurement-related and pertain to goods or services for military agencies, including the Army, Navy, and Air Force. But the government also enters into contracts pertaining to fields of industry or commerce that it regulates. Because the government regulates private concerns in these fields, some contractors lose sight of the fact that the government may, in fact, be contractually obligated to follow certain terms and conditions during the course of its regulatory activities.

It is also good news that our nation increasingly appears to recognize that protecting the sanctity of government contracts is in its own best interest. Twice within the last generation—and not since the *Sinking-Fund Cases* in 1878[4]—once during 1996 in *United States v. Winstar Corporation*[5] and again during 2002 in *Franconia Associates v. United States*,[6] the US Supreme Court has taken great care to reiterate that, once the United States waives its sovereign immunity and does business with its citizens, it does so much as a party never cloaked with immunity: "[t]he United States does business on business terms."[7] In other words, when Uncle Sam chooses to contract with private entities, it subjects itself to the same rules of the road as everyone else. And when Uncle Sam strays from those rules of the road, the federal judiciary is there to steer him back.

---

[4] *Union Pac. R.R. Co. v. United States* (*The Sinking-Fund Cases*), 99 U.S. 700 (1878).
[5] *United States v. Winstar Corp.*, 518 U.S. 839 (1996).
[6] *Franconia Assocs. v. United States*, 536 U.S. 129 (2002).
[7] *Id.* at 141 (quoting *Clearfield Trust Co. v. United States*, 318 U.S. 363, 369 (1943)).

The lawyers at my law firm, Eckland & Blando LLP, were fortunate to persuade the US Supreme Court to rule in favor of its contractor clients in *Franconia Associates.* There, the court held that "[w]e comprehend no reason why an Act of Congress may not constitute a repudiation of a contract to which the United States is a party," and that the subject statute did constitute such a repudiation.[8] At issue were contractual arrangements between owners of low-income housing located in rural areas across the country and the US Department of Agriculture. During oral argument, Justice O'Connor quipped, "the Government should want to have some rules out there that would encourage it to be able to deal with people on a commercial basis."[9] Given the Supreme Court's unanimous ruling in that case, another victory was scored for the enforcement of government contracts.

To date, the law firm of Eckland & Blando LLP has settled significantly more than $300 million worth of similar contract disputes with the government. The teachings of the Supreme Court's opinion in *Franconia Associates*, as well as of other case opinions of its progeny decided by the US Court of Federal Claims, have served the government and its citizens well. The *Franconia Associates* line of cases has assured contractors that, if Uncle Sam goes astray, the federal judiciary will honor those contractual undertakings upon which private business entities are routinely entitled to rely.

Our nation's economy continues to improve while businesses up the ante and negotiate larger and more complex deals with the government. This is not to say that contracting with Uncle Sam has become risk-free. On the contrary, enforcing contractual rights vis-à-vis the federal government sometimes entails finding one's way through what can seem like a veritable thicket of various doctrines in the government's arsenal of defenses. But the *Franconia Associates* line of cases demonstrates that a roadmap for success does exist. One need only know how to navigate the route.

The Regulatory Contract

Interestingly enough, it is easier to define the type of regulatory contract enforceable against Uncle Sam by what it is not, rather than by what it

---

[8] *Id.* at 148.

[9] Transcript of Oral Argument at 54, *Franconia Assocs. v. United States*, 536 U.S. 129 (No. 01-455).

is. A regulatory contract is not a procurement-related contract, which by law is governed by the Contract Disputes Act (CDA) and its unique provisions.[10] Procurement-related contracts are those contracts administered by contracting officers and governed by complex administrative procedures. For example, CDA-covered contracts are governed by such things as the Termination for Convenience (T for C) Clause, which in essence permits the government to breach such contracts for virtually any reason.[11] Contracts subject to the CDA are also governed by the Changes Clause, which provides that "[t]he Contracting Officer may at any time, by written order, and without notice to the sureties, if any, make changes within the general scope of [the] contract . . . ."[12]

> By definition, the CDA governs all contracts entered into by the Government for:
>
> (1) the procurement of property, other than real property;
> (2) the procurement of services;
> (3) the procurement of construction, alteration, repair, or maintenance of real property; or
> (4) the disposal of personal property.[13]

If these are the types of contracts that *are* covered by the CDA, what then, constitutes a contract *not* subject to the CDA? Through a process of elimination, one can set forth the defining characteristics of those contracts that do not fall within the scope of the CDA:

1. Contracts in which the government supplies a service;
2. Agreements by the government arising out of its regulatory activities; and
3. Most implied-in-fact contracts (which by their nature do not have a contracting officer to make the decision that initiates proceedings under the CDA).

[10] Contract Disputes Act, 41 U.S.C. §§ 7101-09 (2011).
[11] *See* 48 C.F.R. § 49.502 (2007).
[12] 48 C.F.R. § 52.243-1 (1987).
[13] 41 U.S.C. § 7102(a)(1)-(4) (2011).

With regard to such "regulatory" contracts not subject to the CDA, the T for C Clause is not applicable. Nor is the Changes Clause applicable. In addition, the terms of such a regulatory contract, like any other commercial contract, do not change with the enactment of subsequent legislation absent a specific contractual provision providing for such a change.[14] Indeed, when the United States enters into such non-CDA contracts, "its rights and duties therein are governed generally by the law applicable to contracts between private individuals."[15] Thus, the government—unlike with regard to CDA contacts containing T for C and/or Changes clauses—may not terminate or change non-CDA contracts for little or no reason. Instead, in the event that the government breaches a regulatory contract, the contractor is entitled to the non-injunctive remedies provided by ordinary contract law—i.e., compensatory damages.

Formation of the Regulatory Contract

Regulatory contracts may look less like contracts than one might think. They do not necessarily consist of one tidy document signed by the contractor, on the one hand, and an authorized representative of the United States, acting in his or her official capacity, on the other. Rather, they may arise out of numerous documents from which, when taken as a whole, one may glean the respective rights and obligations of the signatories thereto. Others may incorporate by reference large swaths of existing regulations or actual statutes. Such contracts may provide that they are *not* subject to future changes in the law that are inconsistent with the contract's terms; others expressly provide that they *are* subject to such changes; still others do not say one way or the other.

In the *Franconia Associates* line of cases, the contracts at issue constituted collections of documents comprising promissory notes, loan agreements, and mortgages. No document alone comprised "the contract." It was necessary to read the separate but related documents together in order to give meaning to the whole contract. This is similar to the case with many

[14] *Conoco Inc. v. United States*, 35 Fed. Cl. 309, 336 (1996), *rev'd on other grounds sub nom. Marathon Oil Co. v. United States*, 177 F.3d 1331 (1999), *rev'd sub nom. Mobile Oil Exploration and Producing Se. Inc. v. United States*, 530 U.S. 604 (2000).
[15] *Franconia Assocs. v. United States*, 536 U.S. 129, 141 (2002) (quoting *Mobile Oil Exploration*, 530 U.S. at 607 (2000)).

other commercial arrangements. One may have standard terms and conditions contained in a purchase agreement here, a seemingly contrary government-authored agreement there, and so on.

Nonetheless, the governing principle for interpreting such contracts is always the same: what is the intent of the parties? Generally, the burden of proof falls upon the party seeking to prove up the contract's terms and conditions to show, first, that a meeting of the minds occurred and, second, what specifically makes up the agreement's terms and conditions. The evidence required to prove up these two factors in the context of government contracts is much the same as that required for commercial contracts. This is one area where the *Franconia Associates* line of cases makes clear that the same governing principles of law apply in both areas.

The best thing a contractor can do for itself at the contracting stage is to ensure that all of its rights and obligations are adequately memorialized in the documentation composing the regulatory contract. Great care should be taken that all of the government's obligations, likewise, are adequately memorialized in writing. This task can be challenging where the regulatory contract may comprise more than one document. Counsel must impress upon contractor clients the need for legal assistance at this early stage. In addition to setting the stage for potential breach of contract actions later, obtaining legal advice at this early stage may avoid the uncertainties that often lead to breaches, thereby obviating the need for litigation altogether.

Uncle Sam's Forfeiture of Immunity for Breach of Contract: The Tucker Act

Prior to 1855, the government enjoyed complete immunity from breach of contract actions. Since the creation of the Court of Claims in 1855, however, the government has been exposed to at least some type of litigation based upon contract disputes:

> The [pre-Civil War waiver of immunity from contract suit] was viewed as indispensable to the efficient operation of government, for without it, qualified private contractors might not undertake government projects

> and the government could not obtain the goods and services it needed at affordable prices.[16]

With the advent of the Tucker Act, what is now called the US Court of Federal Claims acquired "jurisdiction to render judgment upon any claim against the United States founded … *upon any express or implied contract with the United States,* or for liquidated or unliquidated damages in cases not sounding in tort."[17] Moreover, since the advent of the Little Tucker Act, the various district courts of the United States acquired:

> … original jurisdiction, concurrent with the United States Court of Federal Claims, of … [a]ny other civil action or claim against the United States, not exceeding $10,000 in amount, founded … *upon any express or implied contract with the United States,* or for liquidated or unliquidated damages in cases not sounding in tort. …[18]

Unlike in breach of commercial contract actions, however, the only remedy available in contract claims against the federal government is that of compensatory damages: specific performance of contracts generally is not possible against the United States. In practice, however, specific performance is rarely much of a remedy anyway; it is exceedingly difficult, even in commercial cases, to obtain such equitable relief. Courts are nearly as reluctant to award specific performance against a private party as they are against the government—such relief often requires large amounts of judicial resources and sometimes never-ending judicial oversight and is thus, in practice, impractical.

The Sovereign Acts Defense

Governmental conduct that one might not initially suspect could constitute a breach of contract often presents itself as a wolf in sheep's clothing. For example, while legislative acts are virtually always deemed above reproach, the passage of legislation by Congress sometimes entails the impossibility of

[16] Harold J. Krent, *Reconceptualizing Sovereign Immunity*, 45 VAND. L. REV. 1529, 1564-65 (1992).
[17] Tucker Act, 28 U.S.C. § 1491(a)(1) (2011) (emphasis supplied).
[18] Little Tucker Act, 28 U.S.C. §§ 1346(a), (a)(2) (2013) (emphasis supplied).

performance by certain contractors. In the commercial context, this can lead to the invocation of the defense of impossibility. In other words, when Congress enacts a statute that precludes a private contractor from performing a commercial contract with another private contractor, the breaching party is entitled to a defense amounting to "the government made me do it." In many cases, this so-called impossibility defense is an absolute bar to breach of contract liability in litigation between private parties.[19]

Interesting questions arise when the US government constitutes one of the contracting parties. It seems intuitive (and it is) that the impossibility defense remains available to the private contractor when the passage of legislation renders its contract performance to the government unattainable. But what if it is the *government's* performance as contractor that becomes impossible by virtue of its own conduct in passing legislation? Can the government invoke the impossibility defense when its own voluntary action was responsible for rendering its contract performance impossible? One can easily imagine situations where the doctrine of impossibility should be available to the government. But one can just as easily posit other situations where it definitely should not.

Before one can distinguish between those situations where the government should be able to invoke the impossibility defense and those where it should not, one must ask (and answer) an even more basic question: can the passage of legislation by Congress that precludes the performance by the government (in most cases a different branch of government) of a contract to which it is a party constitute a breach of contract by the government? This would appear to constitute a fundamental question crying out for an answer. Yet it is a question that did not receive a definitive answer until the US Supreme Court took it up during 1996 in *Winstar.* The answer was a resounding "yes." There, the court held that the Financial Institutions Reform, Recovery, and Enforcement Act (FIRREA) breached the subject contracts at issue by eliminating the favorable accounting treatment that had been promised to healthy savings and loan institutions that bailed out failing savings and loan institutions.[20]

---

[19] *See generally* RESTATEMENT (SECOND) OF CONTRACTS § 309 (1979).
[20] *Id.* at 909.

The court expounded on its affirmative answer in 2002 when it took up a related but very different question in *Franconia Associates*: can the passage of legislation by Congress that falls short of creating an immediate impossibility of performance, but that rather announces that a promised performance will be unavailable in the future, constitute an "anticipatory repudiation" of contract performance by the government? Again, the court answered with a resounding "yes": "[w]e comprehend no reason why an Act of Congress may not constitute a repudiation of a contract to which the United States is a party."[21] When I was asked during oral argument why such contrary legislation should subject the government to litigation at any point during the entire term of a contract, no matter how long, Justice Scalia abruptly interjected, because *"[t]hat was the deal"* (emphasis supplied).[22]

Now we can return to our original question of how to distinguish between those situations where, when Congress enacts legislation that precludes the government from performing a contract, the government should be able to invoke the impossibility defense and those where it should not. In order to answer this question, one needs to recall that—because of its unique role—the government is often said to wear two hats: "[w]hen sovereign immunity is waived and the sovereign enters the world of contract, it assumes the position of a private person for juridical purposes and yet, in fact, it never leaves behind its sovereign status and its overriding power."[23] Thus, when acting in its capacity as sovereign, the government is entitled to invoke the impossibility defense under the rubric of sovereign immunity.

Such immunity can be justified by the notion that the government should be entitled to the same defense arising from its action as sovereign as would a private contractor that enjoys the impossibility defense resulting from the government's exercise of a sovereign act. For example, if the government

---

[21] *Franconia Assocs. v. United States*, 536 U.S. 129, 148 (2002).

[22] Transcript of Oral Argument at 13, *Franconia Assocs.*, 536 U.S. 129 (No. 01-455) (emphasis supplied).

[23] Gillian Hadfield, *Of Sovereignty and Contract: Damages for Breach of Contract by Government*, 8 S. CAL. INTERDISC. L.J. 467, 472 (1999). *See, also*, URBAN A. LETER & MICHAEL F. NOONE JR., LITIGATION WITH THE FEDERAL GOVERNMENT, § 9.124 (3d ed. 1994) ("The United States, when it makes contracts as a government, is both *contractor* and *sovereign*, and it is held able to act generally, in its capacity as sovereign, without incurring liability for breach of its existing contracts (or for taking of property)" (emphasis supplied)).

imposes an embargo upon the importation of silk in order to protect all US manufacturers from the adverse effects of the silkworm, any manufacturer precluded by the embargo from performing a manufacturing contract utilizing foreign silk is in essence immunized by the doctrine of impossibility. Clearly, the government should be treated no differently in the event that, in its capacity as contractor, it also happens to be precluded by its own embargo from performing a similar manufacturing contract with a commercial entity.

The only difference between these two situations is that the private contractor is said to enjoy the fruits of the doctrine of impossibility, while the government is entitled to invoke the "sovereign acts defense"—as long as the embargo was properly imposed by the government in its capacity as sovereign, rather than in its role as contractor. For if the government can be shown to have improperly imposed the embargo based upon a pretext—such as for the specific purpose of excusing the government from nonperformance of the foreign silk manufacturing contract to which it is a party—then the sovereign acts defense will not apply. The government has acted improperly in its capacity as *contractor,* rather than as in its capacity as *sovereign.*

The main difficulty with the sovereign acts defense lies here—distinguishing between when the defense properly applies and when it does not. In short, governmental acts accomplished for the public welfare are protected by the defense. "Whatever acts the government may do, be they legislative or executive, so long as they be *public and general,* cannot be deemed specially to … violate the particular contracts into which it enters with private persons."[24] The key is whether the act engaged in by the government is, in fact, public and general—i.e., conducted by the government in its sovereign capacity, or whether it is done for reasons specifically related to the contract at issue—i.e., conducted in its capacity as a contractor. Acts that are undertaken in the government's capacity as a contractor, and that interfere with the performance of the contract at issue, are not covered by the sovereign acts defense.[25]

---

[24] *Horowitz v. United States*, 267 U.S. 458, 461 (1925) (quoting *Jones v. United States*, 1 Ct. Cl. 383, 384 (1865) (emphasis supplied)).

[25] *See, e.g.*, *Adams v. United States*, 42 Fed. Cl. 463, 478-80 (Fed. Cl. 1998) (discussing the inapplicability of the sovereign acts defense where legislation is specifically designed to avoid an existing contractual obligation).

In *Franconia Associates*, for example, the trial court ultimately concluded that in passing the legislation at issue, Congress deliberately targeted the government's contractual obligations under pre-existing agreements "in an effort to obtain a better deal than the one [the government had] used to induce plaintiffs to enter into the [low-income housing] program."[26] The more that the government's alleged sovereign acts have "the substantial effect of releasing the Government from its contractual obligations," the more suspect becomes the application of the sovereign acts defense.[27] The government remains liable for breaches of contract resulting from non-sovereign acts.

Unfortunately, distinguishing between an act that is conducted within the government's sovereign capacity, for the public and general welfare (and that therefore is covered by the sovereign acts defense) from an act that is conducted in the government's capacity as a contractor (and that is not so covered) is more difficult in practice than it is in theory. This difficulty arises from the fact that virtually all government conduct presumptively can be argued to be carried out in its sovereign capacity: legislation enacted by Congress—at least on the surface—arguably is calculated to be public and general; executive action undertaken to implement statutory law generally is said to spring from the same motivation; and decisions handed down by the judiciary, albeit limited to the parties before it, also are generally assumed to be rendered in the sovereign capacity of the courts. Nonetheless, the sovereign acts defense is not universally applied—far from it, actually.

Penetrating the cloak of sovereignty in order to discern those governmental acts that are *not* conducted in the general public welfare is possible. It has been accomplished in the past and will be accomplished in the future. And while the task may be somewhat more challenging with regard to the executive than the legislative branch of government, it can be done with regard to both. The task appears easier with regard to the actions of Congress because it consists of a deliberative body. Virtually everything Congress does, it does in public. Committee meetings, Congressional hearings, sessions of the House and the Senate—all are generally conducted in public. And while it would be naïve to believe that absolutely everything that occurs in Congress occurs in public, all substantive Congressional

---

[26] *Franconia Assocs. v. United States*, 61 Fed. Cl. 718, 736 (2004).
[27] *United States v. Winstar Corp.*, 518 U.S. 839, 899 (1996).

decisions ultimately must be subject to the microscope of public scrutiny at some degree of magnitude. Similarly, pursuant to open meeting laws, in theory, most executive decision making must also be conducted in public. And there is something to be said about the fact that determining the true motivations underlying governmental decision making at all levels is easier in our relatively new age of social media.

Pulling back the curtain sometimes requires only that one examine the legislative history of the various statutes as published by the Congressional Record. In the *Franconia Associates* line of cases, for example, the lawyers easily found members of Congress accusing each other of reneging on the contractual obligations of the government. "[I]n legal terms this is called ... an impairment of the obligations of contract. In layman terms it is called welching. Whatever it is, it is basically unfair."[28] Indeed, in our current age of political polarization, determining improper motivations for purposes of determining the applicability of the sovereign acts defense can be as easy as clicking on C-SPAN.

One common element underlying public decision making that is not covered by the sovereign acts defense is the governmental motivation to save money. For better or worse, it is not a sufficient justification for breaching a contract that the governmental body at issue was looking out for the public fisc. Courts almost universally have held that such budget-driven motivations result from conduct arising in the government's capacity as contractor, rather than as sovereign.[29] This may appear counterintuitive to some, and perhaps it is. But this phenomenon is demonstrative of the fact that the sovereign acts defense is not the impenetrable shield that it is perceived by some to be.

Many contractors assume that the sovereign acts defense is impenetrable. That mindset often accompanies the general reluctance of contractors to bring suit against what is often their best customer. What experienced government contractors come to realize, however, is that the powers that be within government recognize that litigation—just as in commercial transactions—is a cost of doing business. Accordingly, the government

---

[28] *Grass Valley Terrace v. United States*, 51 Fed. Cl. 436, 442 (2002) (quoting Congressman Butler, 126 CONG. REC. 22,650 (1980)).

[29] *See, e.g.*, *Gen. Dynamics Corp. v. United States*, 47 Fed. Cl. 514, 542 (2000).

does not begrudge anyone for commencing civil actions against it. Once contractors understand this, they can accept the sovereign acts defense for what it is—simply one weapon among many that the government has in its general arsenal of defenses. And in my experience, the sovereign acts defense is one that the government seems less likely to assert than it traditionally has in the past.

The Unmistakability Doctrine

Another doctrine comes into play in breach of contract actions against the government that has been the subject of much confusion for literally scores of years. It often has been perceived—incorrectly so—as yet another major impediment to the ability to sue Uncle Sam for breach of contract. It is known as the unmistakability doctrine. In its erroneous application, courts have required—as a prerequisite to the government's obligation to perform a contract with a private entity—that the subject contract be written such that there is no question that the government is obligated by the contract's terms. In other words—the argument went—the contract must be written so clearly that it is "unmistakable" in its imposition of contractual obligations upon the government.

One need only recall Justice Holmes's observation that, in the world of government contracts, although "one who deals with the Government may need to 'turn square corners,' ... he need not turn them twice"[30] to recognize that this application of the unmistakability doctrine is incorrect. A contract is a contract—even with the government—and one need not promise twice to make it so. What the erstwhile advocates of this erroneous interpretation have failed to recognize is that the unmistakability doctrine constitutes a shield to governmental liability, not a sword for striking down the enforceability of contracts to which the government is a party.

In short, the doctrine is properly applied only as a means of protecting the government from unintentionally waiving its sovereign acts defense. Before the government can be said to have voluntarily given up its right to invoke the sovereign acts defense, the unmistakability doctrine requires that the government be shown to have intentionally foregone—in unmistakable

[30] *Winstar Corp.*, 518 U.S. at 922 (quoting *Rock Island, A. & L.R. Co. v. United States*, 254 U.S. 141, 143 (1920)).

terms—the right to apply that defense. Thus, in the event that the unmistakability doctrine is applied and an unmistakable waiver of the sovereign acts defense is not found, the government is entitled to raise its shield in the form of that defense. If, however, the sovereign acts defense initially is determined not to apply (for example, if the government's act constitutes a pretext for avoiding a contractual obligation), the unmistakability doctrine has no application. There simply is no sovereign acts defense available for the government to invoke; therefore, no doctrine of unmistakability is necessary to determine whether it has been waived. The unmistakability doctrine cannot, therefore, ever by used as a sword to strike down the enforceability of a contract in the event that the sovereign acts defense does not apply.

Prior to the *Franconia Associates* line of cases, courts often made the mistake of applying the unmistakability doctrine—as a sword—even when the sovereign acts defense had been determined not to apply.[31] Plaintiffs in breach of contract actions were actually required to satisfy an extra burden of proof prior to enforcing contracts against the government. Since the decisions in the *Franconia Associates* and related lines of cases have been rendered, it appears that courts are requiring such an erroneous, extra burden of proof much less frequently where the sovereign acts defense does not apply.

It is only in cases where the sovereign acts defense does apply that a plaintiff must show that the contract—in unmistakable terms—creates a contractual obligation binding upon the government even in the event of subsequent, inconsistent legislation that would otherwise excuse the government's obligation to perform. It is difficult to conceptualize circumstances under which this might occur—i.e., that the government's contractual obligations could ever supersede its sovereign rights. After all,

---

[31] *See, e.g.*, *Grass Valley Terrace v. United States*, 46 Fed. Cl. 629, 637-40 (2000), *aff'd*, 7 F. App'x 928 (Fed. Cir. 2001), *rev'd on other grounds sub nom. Franconia Assocs.*, 536 U.S. 129. Notably, in a decision subsequent to the above-cited decision in *Grass Valley Terrace* (issued before certiorari was granted in *Franconia Associates* in 2002), and while leaving undisturbed its previous holding that the contracts did not constitute unmistakable promises, the COFC reconsidered its prior decision and accepted the argument that, because the legislation at issue did not constitute a sovereign act, the unmistakability doctrine did not bar plaintiffs' claims. *Grass Valley Terrace v. United States*, 51 Fed. Cl. 436, 443 (2002).

we pride ourselves on being a democracy, and in a democracy, Congress generally has the final word.

This is undoubtedly why courts rarely have enforced a contract against the government when the sovereign acts defense does, in fact, apply. It was for this reason that Justice Souter, in his plurality opinion in *Winstar*, skirted the application of the unmistakability doctrine altogether. Instead, he construed the government contract at issue—not as a promise by the government not to enact inconsistent legislation in the future—but rather as a promise to assume the risk that such legislation would be enacted, thereby making the government liable for damages when that legislation was enacted.[32] Justice Scalia, in his concurring opinion in *Winstar*, stated that he would have taken the bull by the horns, maintained that the unmistakability doctrine was none other than an ordinary principle of contract interpretation, and construed the contract as an actual promise by the government not to enact the inconsistent legislation known as FIRREA.[33]

Although the precise meaning of *Winstar*, given these conflicting opinions, is somewhat unclear, what is clear is that, in the event that the unmistakability doctrine is ever satisfied when the sovereign acts defense applies, the plaintiff contractor will be entitled to breach of contract damages. Seen in this proper light, and as discussed above, the unmistakability doctrine is solely a shield against the government's unintentional waiver of the sovereign acts defense. In other words, before the government can be deemed to have surrendered its sovereign right to adversely affect a contractual relationship with a legislative act, it must "unmistakably" have created a contractual obligation that trumps such a sovereign act.

Courts in general began interpreting the interplay between the sovereign acts defense and the unmistakability doctrine properly only during the latter years of the twentieth century. For example, the case of *General Dynamics v. United States* contains an extensive discussion of the relationship between the sovereign acts defense and the unmistakability doctrine.[34] Senior Judge Lydon of the US Court of Federal Claims concluded that a court should

---

[32] *Winstar Corp.*, 518 U.S. at 880.
[33] *Id.* at 921 (Scalia, J. concurring).
[34] *See, generally, Gen. Dynamics Corp.*, 47 Fed. Cl. at 542-44.

first determine whether the legislation was a sovereign act.[35] Next, as described in the *Franconia Associates* line of related cases that implemented Judge Lydon's analysis:

> If [the Sovereign Acts Defense does not apply], then the facts must be analyzed to determine whether the government is bound according to *ordinary* principles of contract law. But if a court concludes that the legislation was a sovereign act, then it must determine whether the government made an *unmistakable* promise to be bound in contract despite subsequent legislative change.[36]

It was left to Judge Allegra of the same court, in his final decision in *Franconia Associates*, to drive the final nail into the coffin that is the erroneous interpretation of the unmistakability doctrine:

> [T]he orbit of [the unmistakability] doctrine significantly intersects that of the sovereign acts doctrine—both apply when the Congress acts to protect public safety, morals or the economy; neither applies when the Congress instead targets the government's contractual obligations in an effort to obtain a better deal.[37]

Thus, when the sovereign acts defense *does* apply, the government's acts taken in its sovereign capacity trump its contractual obligations unless the contract at issue unmistakably waives the sovereign acts defense, (relatedly) otherwise makes clear that the contract unmistakably supersedes future inconsistent legislative change, or operates not as a promise not to enact inconsistent legislation, but rather as a promise by the government to assume the risk that such legislation would be enacted (in which case the government becomes liable for indemnification). When the sovereign acts defense does not apply, however (either because the inconsistent legislation

---

[35] *Id.* at 541 (following *Yankee Atomic Elec. Co. v. United States*, 112 F.3d 1569 (Fed. Cir. 1997).

[36] *Grass Valley Terrace,* 51 Fed. Cl. at 442 (citing *Gen. Dynamics Corp.*, 47 Fed. Cl. at 541 (emphasis supplied)).

[37] *Franconia Assocs.*, 61 Fed. Cl. at 734 (quoting *Cuyahoga Metro. Hous. Auth. v. United States*, 57 Fed. Cl. 751, 774 (2003)).

was improperly designed to relieve the government of its contractual obligations, or if the deemed contractual obligation of indemnification is not made impossible by said legislation), then ordinary private law principles of contract interpretation rule the day, and the unmistakability doctrine has no application whatsoever.

The largest takeaway here for contractors everywhere is quite practical: where the governmental action at issue does not constitute a sovereign act for purposes of a plaintiff's breach of contract claim, a court, following the reasoning of the *Franconia Associates* line of cases, need not proceed to any unmistakability analysis.[38] Ordinary rules of contract interpretation will govern the plaintiff's breach of contract case against the government.

Justice O'Connor's admonishment in *Franconia Associates*—that the federal government should want rules that encourage business between the government and its citizens—applies best to the judiciary's relatively recent reinterpretation of the unmistakability doctrine. Contractors are more likely to contract with Uncle Sam when they can expect the government to honor its bargain, or at least be required to pay compensation for any failure to do so. And the government is more apt to honor its bargain when it understands that the courts will hold the government responsible for its failure to perform its contracts. What contractors are just beginning to understand is that the regulatory contracts into which they enter with the government constitute binding contracts, under ordinary rules of contract interpretation, when the sovereign acts defense does not apply. And even where the defense does apply, opinions such as Justice Scalia's concurring opinion in *Winstar* demonstrate that the unmistakability doctrine no longer constitutes the sharpest tool in the government's cache.

Cooking with Squid: Follow the Recipe because Undercooking or Overcooking Will Give You Nothing

Establishing a breach of contract claim that successfully navigates the sovereign acts defense (by showing either that it does not apply or that, if it does, the government unmistakably has waived its application) or the unmistakability doctrine (by showing that, despite the application of the

[38] *Grass Valley Terrace*, 51 Fed. Cl. at 443.

sovereign acts defense, the subject contract unmistakably trumps the government's sovereign act) is not the be-all and end-all. For once a contractor has circumnavigated these two doctrines, it must also satisfy several other prerequisites for a successful breach of contract claim.

First, the contractor must satisfy the ripeness doctrine—the precept that some governmental action has had a direct impact upon the contract holder. Second, the contractor must satisfy the statute of limitations, which under the Tucker Act is six years after the claim first accrues. (These first two prerequisites can be called the squid factors because, like squid that is cooked too little, a premature claim is no better than no claim at all; and like squid that is cooked too much, a claim submitted after the expiration of the statute of limitations is no good at all.) Finally, the contractor must mitigate its damages, but not to the point of turning the other cheek so many times as to make a fool of itself, like the credulous Charlie Brown trying to kick the football held by the priggish Lucy in the famous *Peanuts* comic strip.

Ripeness

Before a breach of contract claim is actionable, it must be ripe. That is, the action or conduct at issue must have had a direct, adverse effect on the contract holder.[39] For example, in those instances where the breach at issue is precipitated by the enactment of a statute or the promulgation of a regulation, actionable effects do not occur unless the implementation of the law has had a direct effect on the contract holder. The mere passage of the statute or promulgation of the regulation, unless they have immediate effects, is insufficient to constitute an actionable breach.

In practice, this often entails that actionable conduct does not occur until a government employee's decision directly affects a contract holder. Another way of expressing this is that actionable conduct does not occur until the application of a government policy is made that directly affects a contract holder. If a breach of contract action is brought prematurely, it is not likely to be dismissed. This is because, although a breach has not technically occurred, the contract can be said to have been repudiated. An action for anticipatory

---

[39] *See Nat'l Park Hospitality Ass'n v. Dept. of Interior*, 538 U.S. 803, 807-08 (2003).

repudiation of a contract can be commenced well before the actual breach has occurred. The practical problem with such an action, however, is that it may be difficult in some cases to assess compensatory damages where the conduct at issue has not yet had a direct effect on the contract holder.

Statute of Limitations

The flip side of the coin is that, in the event that a contract holder waits too long before commencing an action for breach of contract, the injured party may become subject to the statute of limitations. In breach of actions against the government pursuant to the Tucker Act, the statute of limitations period is six years from the date that the claim first accrues.[40]

The key issue is when a claim first accrues for the purposes of the statute of limitations. The short answer is that a claim for breach of contract first accrues when a breach occurs. Thus, the statute of limitations does not begin to run unless the time for performance arrives and the government fails to perform. Although a claim for anticipatory repudiation may be commenced before that time, such a claim is not subject to the statute of limitations. Otherwise, claimants would be compelled to file suit prematurely—well before the actual breach accrues—for fear that they would otherwise relinquish their claims by reason of the expiration of the statute of limitations.[41] Rather, the statute of limitations commences to run only as of the time that the government action at issue directly and adversely affects the contractor.

Mitigation of Damages

The doctrine of mitigation of damages is familiar to most. It requires that one must engage in conduct reasonably calculated to lessen the adverse impact that the breaching party's conduct has had on the plaintiff.[42] However, the law of private contract has developed another, lesser known, corollary to the mitigation doctrine that essentially holds that one is not obligated to continue to deal with a breaching party. "Courts generally have held that it is not necessary for the plaintiff to make another contract with

[40] 28 U.S.C. § 2501 (2004).
[41] *See Franconia Assocs. v. United States*, 536 U.S. 129, 143 (2002).
[42] *See, generally,* RESTATEMENT (SECOND) OF CONTRACTS § 350 (1981).

the defendant who has repudiated, even though he offers terms that would result in avoiding loss."[43] Stated otherwise, "an innocent party is not [automatically] required to execute a less advantageous contract with one who has *already welshed* on his agreement."[44]

The key question for our analysis, of course, is whether this corollary doctrine applies to the world of government contracts. Fortunately, it does.[45] This is important, especially considering the pervasive influence the government has over people's lives. Thus, the notion that one must "turn the other cheek" in the face of government misconduct simply does not apply after a certain point. In practice, this means that following the government's breach of a contract, one is not compelled to enter into a less advantageous contract with the government.

This is true even though the government may claim that such action is required. "Accordingly, courts have been reluctant to require parties, under the duty to mitigate, to deal further with the breaching party. ..."[46] "Colloquially speaking, the law of mitigation does not require plaintiffs to play the role of the credulous Charlie Brown to the [government's] priggish Lucy, in recreating the Schulzian football-kicking scenario that always finds poor Charlie on his back."[47]

During the course of performance of regulatory contracts, several steps should be taken by the contractor to ensure that a breach of contract is detected when it occurs, that any claim for breach of contract does not become too stale to assert, and that the contractor does not go overboard in its attempts to placate its government customer. First, contractors and their counsel should periodically review governmental conduct to identify any action that is inconsistent with the government's contractual obligations. Any such improper governmental conduct should be brought to the attention of senior-level management as soon as practically possible. Such governmental behavior needs to be examined by experienced counsel to determine whether any actionable conduct has occurred.

---

[43] JOSEPH M. PERILLO, CORBIN ON CONTRACTS § 57.15 (rev. ed. 2005).
[44] *Cain v. Grosshans & Petersen Inc.*, 413 P.2d 98, 102 (Kan. 1966) (emphasis supplied).
[45] *See, generally, Franconia Assocs.*, 536 U.S. 129.
[46] *Koby v. United States*, 53 Fed. Cl. 493, 497 (2002).
[47] *Franconia Assocs.*, 61 Fed. Cl. at 742.

Second, some kind of tickler system should be devised and implemented in order to ensure that any viable claims for breach of contract do not expire for failure to satisfy the statute of limitations. The limitations period for breach of contract claims against Uncle Sam—six years—may at first blush seem a long time, but it often passes by in the blink of an eye. It makes a great deal of sense to re-visit the conduct at issue in one-year increments in order to re-evaluate the nature of the breach and its consequences for the contractor's performance and the bottom line. That way, the contractor never loses sight of the resulting issues and can periodically re-assess whether a civil action for breach of contract against the government makes economic sense.

Third, regular meetings with counsel regarding the degree to which mitigation may be required are highly recommended. Mitigating conduct that does not further obligate the contractor is not only a good idea, but it may also be required. Not only may it be required, but it also may be a necessary prerequisite for the successful recovery of breach of contract damages. Identifying where to draw the line between mitigating conduct that does not go far enough and that which may go too far is always difficult to do. Indeed, such line-drawing is at least as difficult as cooking squid.

Conclusion

More than 150 years ago, Congress saw fit to abolish the sovereign immunity enjoyed by the United States in breach of contract actions. At the time, this action was seen as essential to the encouragement of commerce with the federal government. In the intervening years, however, the sanctity of contract often was more observed in the breach than in the observance. That was until the US Supreme Court—in a decision at the dawn of this century giving rise to a line of cases known as *Franconia Associates*—saw fit once again to sanctify the observance of contracts between the government and its citizens.

It continues to be up to each of us as citizens of the United States to put that idealism into practice—to fulfill the mandate that our word is our bond, to hold the government accountable for the contracts it makes with each of us, and to not shrink from our duty to show Uncle Sam the way forward. For it is only by doing so that each of us can ensure that our joint efforts will help safeguard the continued economic success of a great commercial nation.

Key Takeaways

- Inform contractors that the more that the government's alleged sovereign acts have the substantial effect of releasing the government from its contractual obligations, the more suspect becomes the application of the sovereign acts defense and therefore the more likely that the government will be held responsible for breach of contract.
- Inform contractors that where the governmental conduct at issue does not constitute a sovereign act for purposes of a plaintiff's breach of contract claim, a court, following the reasoning of the *Franconia Associates* line of cases, need not proceed to any unmistakability analysis, and contracts will be enforced under ordinary rules of contract interpretation.
- Keep in mind that before a breach of contract claim is actionable, it must be ripe. That is, the action or conduct at issue must have had a direct, adverse effect on the contract holder.
- Note that in the event that a contract holder waits too long before commencing an action for breach of contract, the injured party may be non-suited for being too late pursuant to the statute of limitations.
- Advise clients that following the government's breach of a contract, one is not compelled to enter into a less advantageous contract with the government.

Jeff H. Eckland, partner with Eckland & Blando LLP, focuses his practice on government contract and general commercial litigation. He has litigated cases in state and federal trial courts across the country, the US Court of Federal Claims, the Boards of Contract Appeals, and numerous state and federal appellate courts. Before the US Supreme Court, he successfully argued that when the government enters into business deals with the private sector, it must play by the same rules that apply to its citizens. Franconia Assocs. v. United States, 536 U.S. 129 (2002). *At the ensuing trial, the government was ordered to pay the plaintiffs more than $13 million in damages.*

Acknowledgment: *I gratefully acknowledge Gregory L. Singleton and Jared M. Reams, associates at Eckland & Blando LLP, for their work proofing this chapter's footnotes. I also thank Gregory L. Singleton and Mark J. Blando, my law partner, for their helpful comments on a draft of this chapter.*

Dedication: *To the memory of James L. "Jim" Poehlman, citizen, client, and friend, without whose wise heart and encouragement* Franconia Associates *would never have been decided.*

Successfully Representing Contractor Clients in Government Contract Claims

Joseph McManus

Partner

McManus Darden & Felsen LLP

ASPATORE

Introduction

In this chapter, I discuss changes in the landscape of government contract law, particularly since the economic downturn of 2008. As the Federal Acquisition Regulation (FAR) has been revised and the burden of proof increasingly favors the government, contractors less acquainted with the federal contracting arena have encountered lower profit margins, and recently, claims, as well as requests for equitable adjustment, have proliferated.

Changes to the standard operating procedures and practices have been observed in the behavior of both government agencies and contractors. On the government side, the most notable shifts are the Department of Justice's increased use of False Claims Act defenses and the prolific rise and successful use of alternative dispute resolution (ADR) tools, such as mediation, in the Court of Federal Claims and the agency Boards of Contract Appeals. For contractors, the use of programs such as Contractor Performance Assessment Reports System (CPARS) may influence litigation strategy and an increased propensity to seek a negotiated solution through a contracting officer, rather than in the Court of Federal Claims or the Boards of Contract Appeals.

For contractors—and their attorneys—to successfully navigate this changing landscape, it is critical that they acquire a working familiarity with the concepts and evolutions described in this chapter.

Recent Trends in the Government Contracts Arena

Among the recent trends that I have observed in the government contracts arena is the increasing aggressiveness of the Department of Justice (DOJ) when it comes to pursuing claims brought under the False Claims Act.[1] Years ago, I enjoyed bringing my cases to the Court of Federal Claims rather than certain Boards of Contract Appeals. At that time, the Justice Department Civil Division was lean. The Court of Claims (as it was then called) had a small bar. I believe that there was a level of mutual respect between government contract law practitioners coming

[1] False Claims Act, 31 U.S.C. §§ 3729-3733 (2012).

before the Justice Department bar; basically, the Justice Department assumed that I was not going to take on a claim that I did not think I could successfully advance to the Court of Federal Claims. Indeed, soon after a case was filed, the lawyers were typically able to sit down and discuss the merits of the case—i.e., why it was filed—in an open and frank way. Again, because it was a small bar, credibility was key, and we were able to settle many cases out of court. It was a more practical environment than the one we are dealing with today.

Currently, there is much fear involved when it comes to going to the Court of Federal Claims because of the knee-jerk reaction to assert a counterclaim that the Justice Department believes it may have with respect to the claim you are bringing.[2] One notable case involving a counterclaim was *Daewoo Eng'g and Constr. Ltd. v. US*,[3] where the government was awarded more than $50 million on its counterclaim. A strong claim is normally a successful claim, and, conversely, because of the increased focus that the Justice Department is exerting in this area these days, one would be foolish to take a claim that was not completely meritorious before the court.

Looking forward, I believe that lawyers in this area will have to make a serious decision as to whether they want to bring a government contracts case to the appropriate Board of Contract Appeals or the Court of Federal Claims and consider the strengths and weaknesses of each venue. For instance, I worked with the Armed Services Board of Contract Appeals (ASBCA) as an Air Force JAG officer from 1972 to 1976, and I have found that the Armed Services Board has maintained a high level of quality with respect to its decision making and objectivity. Its judges are all trained government contract lawyers. If government contract experience is essential to your case, the boards may weigh in your favor. On the other hand, not all of the judges at the Court of Federal Claims are government contract lawyers; additionally, the trend these days is for the Justice Department to raise a False Claims Act defense and counterclaim.

---

[2] For further explanation of the DOJ's use of counterclaims, *see* Matthew Solomson, *When the Government's Best Defense Is a Good Offense; Litigating Fraud and Other Counterclaim Cases before the U.S. Court of Federal Claims*, BRIEFING PAPERS, November 2011.

[3] *Daewoo Eng'g & Constr. Ltd. v. United* States, 73 Fed. Cl. 547 (2006).

Another interesting trend in this area is the change that was made to the FAR—i.e., certain incurred costs in relation to a contract are no longer deemed reasonable. Previously, if you had incurred costs in the course of executing a government contract, it was presumed by the Defense Contract Audit Agency (DCAA), the Court of Federal Claims, and the Board of Contract Appeals that the costs were reasonable—otherwise, why would you incur them?[4] However, there is now no presumption of reasonability associated with any of the costs in this area; FAR 31.201-3 establishes the criteria for determining reasonableness.[5]

Use of ADR in Government Contracts Litigation

I have found that many of the recent trends in government contracts litigation follow the recent trends in the commercial world, where ADR is dominant. Indeed, when you take a case to the Board of Contract Appeals or the Court of Federal Claims, there will be a push by the court or the board for you to go to mediation to try to get the matter resolved. I think that is a good idea; certainly, if you have a solid, valid claim, you should be more than happy to talk with representatives from the government contracting agency.

---

[4] "Previously, a contractor's incurred costs were entitled to a presumption of reasonableness, and the Government bore the burden of proving that the costs were unreasonable. This presumption, however, was superseded in 1987 by an amendment to FAR 31.201-3." *Kellogg Brown & Root Serv. Inc. v. United States*, 107 Fed. Cl. 16, 39 (2012) (internal citation omitted).

[5] FAR 31.201-3.Determining Reasonableness.

(a) A cost is reasonable if, in its nature and amount, it does not exceed that which would be incurred by a prudent person in the conduct of competitive business. Reasonableness of specific costs must be examined with particular care in connection with firms or their separate divisions that may not be subject to effective competitive restraints. No presumption of reasonableness shall be attached to the incurrence of costs by a contractor. If an initial review of the facts results in a challenge of a specific cost by the contracting officer or the contracting officer's representative, the burden of proof shall be upon the contractor to establish that such cost is reasonable.

(b) What is reasonable depends upon a variety of considerations and circumstances, including --

(1) Whether it is the type of cost generally recognized as ordinary and necessary for the conduct of the contractor's business or the contract performance;

(2) Generally accepted sound business practices, arm's-length bargaining, and Federal and State laws and regulations;

(3) The contractor's responsibilities to the Government, other customers, the owners of the business, employees, and the public at large; and

(4) Any significant deviations from the contractor's established practices.

Other forms of ADR, such as early neutral evaluation, have been used less frequently. Some prove to be effective. For example, early neutral evaluation can be a successful tool in a mammoth case where you have hundreds of millions of dollars at stake and the parties are poles apart. The recent article by Judge Williams and Judge Page found that the success rate in mediation using ASBCA judges is well over 95 percent,[6] and that result speaks legions for its effectiveness. However, a government agency can be intransigent for whatever reason and force you to go to the limits of litigation. It may be, for example, that the resident engineer is so far invested in unwise contract management that he or she has lost objectivity.

Industries or Service Sectors Litigating Government Contracts

It appears that government contract cases (protests and claims) involving the information technology (IT) industry have become more common in recent times, and we are seeing recently more cases involving the service and construction industries. More people got into the federal contracting arena when the economy started to shrink—and many of those people were unprepared for the regulations and standard form contract constraints that exist in this area. Profit margins became thin, and losses mounted, which, in turn have since given rise to more claims.

It should be noted that the ASBCA publishes statistics on appeals docketed, decisions where the board found merit, appeals dismissed, and other information, and that information can often be helpful. [7]

Successfully Litigating Government Contracts

In order to successfully litigate a government contract, you need to know the contract provisions backwards and forwards and the provisions of the FAR in relation to the contract. It is also important to have a good handle on any costs you are likely to incur. As soon as the contractor realizes that there may be a problem, the contractor should make sure it is keeping track of its costs and

---

[6] Reba Ann Page & Paul Williams, *The ASBCA's Path to the "Mega ADR" in Computer Sciences Corporation*, THE PROCUREMENT LAW., Fall 2013, at 1.

[7] *Quarterly and Annual Reports*, ARMED SERVICES BOARD OF CONT. APPEALS, http://www.asbca.mil/Reports/reports.html (last visited Sept. 17, 2014).

time for a potential claim. The client should obtain good legal and financial advice from an expert before it starts advancing requests for equitable adjustment or claims in this arena. The heart of claims is in the contract's changes clause—a contractor must be skilled in knowing the landscape of a bilateral change, a unilateral change, and a constructive change.[8]

Most important, a client needs to consult a skilled, experienced government contracts lawyer who can tell whether it has a valid claim. For instance, I get a number of referrals from very well-known construction lawyers who do not venture into the government contracts arena frequently or at all. It important for the client to hire a person with substantial knowledge of and experience in government contracts law. You would not venture into a government contract case with your trademark lawyer, even though your trademark lawyer may be your outside general counsel.

I do not feel that there are any significant differences in litigation strategies among contract types (supply, service, construction, etc.). Again, it is critical to know your contract, its operative clauses, and the FAR regulations. Of course, there may be some differences in litigation strategies for other reasons. As an example, you may want to be less aggressive when you have a large, multi-year option contract.

Likewise, construction contractors should be aware of CPARS, which assesses a contractor's performance at the end of the contract period. For instance, if you become known as a litigious contractor whose behavior is affecting the procurement officers you are dealing with, you may find yourself with a low CPARS rating—and that situation will often dictate a litigation strategy in terms of trying to get disputes resolved at the contracting officer level, rather than pushing them toward litigation. You can litigate the reasonableness of the rating with the board or with the Court of Federal Claims, but they have no jurisdiction to order the agency to change the rating. Thus, for example, if the rating is of concern, the contractor may want to consider also advancing an unrelated but fully supportable monetary claim and take them together to the court or board and seek to negotiate them both at the same time.

---

[8] *See* Joe McManus and Karlee Blank, *Claim Identification and Notification, in* CONSTRUCTION CONTRACT CLAIMS, CHANGES & DISPUTE RESOLUTION (Paul Levin ed., 2d ed. forthcoming 2014).

The Role of the Client and Experts in Supplying Information for the Litigation Strategy

It is extremely important for a client in a government contracting case to maintain control over its documents—and that includes any electronic documents, which can be highly significant in discovery. Basically, the client needs to know what is in its files and what information is deleted as a routine business practice. Clients should be counseled on corporate document destruction policy. You need to obtain that information from the client early in the case. E-mails make for sloppy authors.

Experts can also contribute significantly to developing a case strategy in this area. That is the reason I am a proponent of early expert involvement in these cases—including initially hiring a non-testifying consultant into my law firm. For example, I might hire a cost expert to conduct some early evaluation on the client's cost management system and on initial claim pricing, and a scheduling consultant to do an early evaluation of schedule creation, approval, and management and the support for a delay claim. Additionally, if I am dealing with a massive job involving the production of millions of documents, it is a good idea to get a document control specialist involved early to evaluate the magnitude of the situation and talk to the client about how its documents are stored in preparation for document production and how to control that process.

You also need to decide how to package your claim. For example, you may have a client who was diligent with neither notice nor documenting the costs incurred with respect to constructive changes. Failure to give notice, if it is prejudicial to the government, could be fatal to the client's claim. In some cases, rather than advancing these otherwise valid individual claims, you may be able to present a modified total cost claim. For example, a new entrant into the government contracting arena may have been "accommodating" to the resident engineer and failed to give notice of a claim and failed to properly segregate costs. Government contracts is a world of notice and protection of rights in writing by both sides. Essentially, attorneys must have a very firm understanding of what happened in their clients' cases so that they can package their claims correctly.

Alternatives to Litigation

Clearly, negotiation is the first stage in any government contracts claims matter—but it is important to keep in mind that times have changed in this area. For example, years ago, if you were working on an Army Corps of Engineers job, your contracting officer was likely to be a senior, crusty colonel, and in order to deal with a claim in that kind of environment, you would have needed to put together a highly coherent package. Essentially, your claim would be packaged with an introduction and a description of the contract, a description of what happened during the contracting process, and then a legal analysis as to why your client is entitled to money, followed by a detailed and comprehensive statement of costs/damages. You would have submitted this document to the contracting officer, and typically, the next step would have been to sit down with the colonel in a job site trailer and negotiate the claim to conclusion before you left the trailer.

These days, while the nature of contracting officers has changed in certain respects, it is still important to meet with the contracting officer and discuss a possible resolution. It may be that the contracting officer—unlike the crusty colonel of years ago—has little familiarity with what has actually happened during the course of the project because a contracting officer's representative (COR) was actually running the project. Therefore, in some cases, the contracting officer is hearing the true facts of the case for the first time at the claim stage. Alternatively, you can request mediation with the Armed Services Board at any stage of your claim. For instance, the client's claim may not have risen to the level of a Contract Disputes Act (CDA)[9]-certified claim; it may just be a Request for an Equitable Adjustment (REA). In such cases, the Board of Contract Appeals, at the request of the parties, can still assist you in getting your claim resolved.

Filing Requirements when Litigating Government Contracts

Obviously, you cannot close out a contract and keep pursuing claims. Particularly as the project nears the point of substantial completion, the contractor must be keenly aware of any potential claims situations and make

[9] Contracts Disputes Act of 1978, Pub. L. No. 95-563, 92 Stat. 2383.

a timely decision on whether to pursue REAs or other claims. The reason for this is that the contractor must submit an REA or a claim to the contracting officer *before* the agency tenders the final payment for a project. Several provisions of the FAR reiterate this point. The FAR's differing site conditions provision, for example, states that "[n]o request by the Contractor for an equitable adjustment to the contract for differing site conditions shall be allowed if made after final payment under this contract."[10] Upon receipt of final payment for the project, the contractor cannot assert additional claims or make new requests for equitable adjustment. Do not invoice for the entire remaining contract balance.

At the same time, there is a generous six-year deadline to initiate a claim and no requirement that you first submit it as an REA—such a request can be made at any time during the course of the job. For instance, it can be submitted promptly after you have already given notice of the claim.

It should be noted that an REA does not include interest, as does a certified claim, but at the same time, if you submit an REA, you may be able to recover legal and consultant fees that you expended when putting it together. On the other hand, after you submit a certified claim, you can no longer claim any costs incurred in pursuit of that claim.

Also, there is no rushed time restraint on when to submit an REA or a certified claim. As a general rule, the most important deadline to bear in mind in a claims situation is the six-year "presentation period," which effectively operates as a six-year statute of limitations for federal contract claims.[11] Contractors must *present* a claim within six years from the date a claim *accrues*.[12] A claim's "accrual" refers to "the date when all events, that fix the alleged liability of either the Government or the contractor and permit assertion of the claim, were known or should have been known."[13]

---

[10] FAR 52.236-2(d).

[11] *See, e.g.*, 41 U.S.C. § 7103(a)(4)(A) ("Each claim by a contractor against the Federal Government relating to a contract and each claim by the Federal Government against a contractor relating to a contract shall be submitted within 6 years after the accrual of the claim").

[12] *Uniglobe Gen. Trading & Contracting Co. v. United States*, 107 Fed. Cl. 423, 431 (2012).

[13] FAR 33.201.

Obviously, there are some notice provisions in a contract that have time-related requirements. For example, with respect to a change conditions clause, you are supposed to notify the government within a certain period after you discover the changed condition—but, again, REAs and certified claims do not have that requirement. The key deadline to keep in mind for the latter category of claims is that they must be brought within six years of their accrual and presented to the contracting officer before the agency tenders final payment on the project.

Working with Experts, Other Lawyers, and Government Agencies

Many people are involved in the government contracts litigation process. For example, while the legal team manages the process, I will also consult with non-testifying experts whom I cannot put on the witness stand. Basically, these experts are working as an arm of the legal team, and that means that the work product that we develop as a team is privileged. Such experts are able to advise us on strategy and tactics in their particular discipline, such as scheduling or cost consulting. I also like to consult with a good practical expert in the particular arena my client may be involved in—i.e., an electrical or structural issue. Likewise, a document control specialist can be a good part of the team if the number of documents in the case is extensive, and the specialist's assistance ensures confidentiality and efficiency.

When working with a government agency during the litigation process, communication is key. Very often when you are in a claim situation, there is some type of barrier that prevents effective communication between the contractor and the contracting officer or its representative. It may be that both parties are working on a particularly tough project, and many change orders were initiated. In other cases, deficiencies may have arisen for which neither the government nor the contractor was responsible—for example, bad engineering by a third party. Therefore, you should look for opportunities to have discussions with executives who go beyond (and above) the parties who are actually constructing a particular project.

I also like to reach out early to the lawyers on the other side, and in some cases, an executive within the client-company needs to have a conversation with a senior-level government agency official. It is important to keep in mind that senior-level agency officials are also business people, and they want competition in terms of contractors bidding on their next job. A contractor executive who thinks that he or she is being abused may not bid on another job that is offered by that particular agency. The meetings between these senior-level parties do not need to involve their lawyers; they can occur in a settlement or compromise environment.

Common Obstacles

One of the biggest obstacles to settling these cases occurs when the parties have vested positions. For instance, let us say that the government contracting officer may not have obtained good legal advice before he or she took a particular position—e.g., the contracting officer may believe that he or she was just deducting certain work from the contract and issued a deductive change order—but the language and the vehicle used created a termination for convenience. Such a mistake has massive repercussions because in a deductive change order, you are pricing the value of any deleted work; whereas, when you are using a termination of convenience, your contract is converted to a cost contract.[14] We are then in an entirely different section of FAR. FAR 52.249-2 Termination for Convenience of the Government (Fixed-Price) (or a similar FAR clause, depending on the type of contract) governs the procedures for determining the amount owed to the contractor. Following termination, the contractor submits a termination settlement proposal to the government, and under Alternate 1 (September 1996), which applies to construction contracts, if the parties cannot agree on the amount due the contractor, the government pays the contractor based on the cost of the work and other factors, such as profit and the cost of subcontractors' termination settlements.

It could be that the government official took a certain position based on the belief that the exposure of the government was X, when, in fact, it was X+ Y + Z; therefore, he or she is locked into a position of inability to negotiate and needs to put the dispute into someone else's hands to get it resolved and/or push it downstream.

[14] "As a general proposition, a fixed price contract is converted into a cost reimbursement contract once it is terminated for convenience and the contractor is entitled to recover, inter alia, its allowable costs incurred in performance of the terminated contract." Worsham Constr. Co., ASBCA No. 25907, 85-s BCA P 18016, 1985 WL 16693 (internal citations omitted).

Conversely, the contractor may be a neophyte to government contracting, and even though it was supposed to give notice of any changes that were occurring or events that rose to the level of constructive changes, it did not do so. This lack of notice prejudiced the government because if the government had known what had happened, it would have altered its position—or at least, that is what its testimony would reveal. Lack of notice is normally the first line of defense by the government, but it is not generally successful unless there is prejudice involved. However, if there is prejudice involved, then that position or the lack of position taken by the contractor could be fatal. The contractor may be sincere and accurate in its belief that the government caused all of the damages involved in its claim, but at the same time, it may not appreciate what effect its lack of notice has had on the claim itself. Simply put, positions taken by both sides could prove to be significant impediments to getting issues resolved.

Conclusion: Impacts of the Current Budget Climate on the Government's Contracting Process

While we thought defense spending would decrease, it is now likely that we will see a significant rise in government defense contract spending over the next few years, based on what is going on in the Middle East. On the other hand, it is almost impossible to predict how much money is going to be spent on federal government contracts going forward because changes in this area occur rapidly. Spending is reactive. The Veterans Administration (VA) has had to increase its budget substantially for basic veterans' care and construction of new facilities because of the scandals that have come to light with respect to the care it was providing. General Services Administration (GSA) construction is in decline. Public-private partnerships (PPPs) are on the rise in infrastructure and transportation. Wastewater treatment plants have deteriorated, and Environmental Protection Agency (EPA) spending will increase.

As noted, when the general economy is going through bad times, more people will compete for government contracts—and unfortunately, the profit margin for a contractor was much higher a few years ago than it is now. Also, many contractors who are new to this area do not realize that they are facing a different structure from the structure that exists in the commercial arena. They are going in with low margins, and they do not know what they are doing; they may find themselves well behind the cash curve. Certain rules have to be followed and notice letters have to be sent. My advice to other government contract attorneys who want to improve the outcome of litigation for their clients is to know the FAR and the contract you are dealing with, as noted, as well as the relevant case law. You will substantially increase your chances with regard to successfully litigating cases with the US government and getting a solid result short of litigation.

Key Takeaways

- Know your client's contract provisions, as well as the provisions of the FAR in relation to the contract. Have a good handle on any costs you are likely to incur. Ensure that you know the contract's changes clause—and the laws that define a bilateral change, a unilateral change, and a constructive change. Advise the client to obtain good legal and financial advice from an expert before advancing claims in this arena. The False Claims Act is a terrorizing piece of legislation.
- Ensure that the client maintains control over its documents. Basically, the client needs to know what is in its files and what information is deleted as a routine business practice—and you need to obtain that information from the client early in the case.
- Decide how to package your claim. For example, you may have a client who has not been documenting the costs incurred with respect to constructive changes, or who has failed to give notice of a change—which, if it is prejudicial to the government, could be fatal to its claim. In some cases, rather than advancing a series of constructive changes, you may be able to advance a modified total cost claim.
- Hire experts who are able to advise you on strategy and tactics in their particular disciplines, such as scheduling or cost consulting. Also consult with a good practical expert as a non-testifying expert in the particular arena your client may be involved in—e.g., an electrical or structural issue. Likewise, a document control specialist can be a good part of the litigation team if the number of electronic documents in the case is extensive.

Joseph McManus, a partner in the firm of McManus Darden & Felsen LLP, advises clients on construction and commercial issues and disputes. He gained this experience as a construction and public contracts lawyer since 1972, as a lawyer in the US Air Force Judge Advocate General Corps assigned to the Armed Services Board of Contract Appeals (ASBCA), as general counsel to Clark Enterprises Inc. (parent of Clark Construction Inc.), and as a member of his own firm. He has also represented many public owners, including Metropolitan Washington Airports Authority, the District of Columbia Council, the government of Barbados, and the government of Greece.

Mr. McManus frequently serves as arbitrator on local, national, and international cases. He is a member of the Large Complex Case Panel of Arbitrators and a mediator (American Arbitration Association). He has appeared as an expert witness in cases involving construction documents in the United States and in the Caribbean. Mr. McManus is a past president of the American College of Construction Lawyers.

APPENDIX

107 FED.CL. 16

United States Court of Federal Claims.

KELLOGG BROWN & ROOT SERVICES, INC., Plaintiff,

v.

The UNITED STATES, Defendant.

Nos. 09–428C, 09–578C.

Sept. 27, 2012.

Background: Contractor brought action against United States to recover costs for the provision of dining facility services in Iraq that were passed through to it under fixed-price contracts.

Holdings: The Court of Federal Claims, Miller, J., held that:

(1) prime contractor failed to show that it employed sound business practices and acted as a reasonably prudent business in accepting subcontractor's proposed prices for one change order, and
(2) was entitled to reimbursement of costs paid to subcontractor in change order providing a new SOW (statement of work) band pricing structure.

Order in accordance with opinion.

West Headnotes

[1] Public Contracts 316H 415(2)

316H Public Contracts

316HX Rights and Remedies of Contractors

316Hk409 Remedies of Contractors

316Hk415 Evidence

316Hk415(2) k. Presumptions and burden of proof. Most Cited Cases

United States 393 74(10)

393 United States

393III Contracts

393k74 Rights and Remedies of Contractors

393k74(10) k. Evidence in general. Most Cited Cases

Contractor, which sought reimbursement of costs incurred in connection with provision of dining facility services for the United States Army in Iraq, had burden of proving by a preponderance of evidence the reasonableness of its claimed costs.

[2] Public Contracts 316H 278

316H Public Contracts

316HV Construction and Operation

316Hk278 k. Change in plans. Most Cited Cases

United States 393 70(25.1)

393 United States

393III Contracts

393k70 Construction and Operation of Contracts

393k70(25) Changes in Plans; Directions or Approval of Officer

393k70(25.1) k. In general. Most Cited Cases

Prime contractor failed to show that it employed sound business practices and acted as a reasonably prudent business in accepting subcontractor's proposed prices for change order issued in connection with provision of dining facility services in Iraq, and therefore contractor was not entitled to reimbursement of those costs which were passed through to it under change order.

[3] Public Contracts 316H 278

316H Public Contracts

316HV Construction and Operation

316Hk278 k. Change in plans. Most Cited Cases

United States 393 70(25.1)

393 United States

393III Contracts

393k70 Construction and Operation of Contracts

393k70(25) Changes in Plans; Directions or Approval of Officer

393k70(25.1) k. In general. Most Cited Cases

Given that its position previously had been that payment was to be made in accordance with the SOW (statement of work) capacity figure, prime contractor, which contracted for provision of dining facility services in Iraq, acted reasonably when faced with a sudden increase in capacity in wartime environment due to troop surge and was entitled to reimbursement of costs paid to subcontractor in change order providing a new SOW bandpricing structure; contractor's approach of creating a new headcount band was reasonable in the circumstances where prices in the new band were derived by computing an incremental increase from the prices in the existing headcount bands that were established competitively.

***17** James J. Gallagher, Los Angeles, CA, for plaintiff. Sandra B. Wick Mulvany and Phillip R. Seckman, McKenna Long & Aldridge LLP, Denver, CO, of counsel.

J. Reid Prouty, Washington, DC, with whom was Acting Assistant Attorney General Stuart F. Delery, for defendant. Renee Gerber, of counsel.

MEMORANDUM OPINION AND ORDER

MILLER, Judge.

This case involves a claim for the provision of dining facility services for the United States Army at Camp Anaconda, one of the largest United States military bases in Iraq during the troop buildup following the March 2003 invasion. Its resolution calls for reconciliation of the prime contractor's burden to provide reasonable justification—years after the fact—for claimed costs that were passed through to the prime contractor under fixed-price contracts with the reality that the costs were incurred during the exigencies of war.

FACTS[1]

Background

<u>The LOGCAP III Contract</u>

In connection with the Government's Logistics Civil Augmentation Program ("LOGCAP"), in December 2001, the United States Army (the "Army") awarded Contract No. DAAA09–02–D–0007 (the "LOGCAP III

[1] The facts set forth in the "Facts" and "Discussion" sections of this opinion constitute the court's findings of fact pursuant to RCFC 52(a)(1), (c). Rulings on mixed questions of fact and law also are set forth in the "Discussion" section.

Contract" or the "Contract") to Brown and Root Services, Inc., a division of Kellogg Brown & Root, Inc. Joint Stipulation filed Dec. 2, 2011, ¶ 1 ("Jt. Stipl. I"); JX 2, at 7590. On August 1, 2003, the LOGCAP III Contract was novated from Brown and Root Services, Inc., to Kellogg Brown & Root Services, Inc. ("KBR" or "plaintiff"). Jt. Stipl. I ¶ 1. The LOGCAP III Contract was a cost-plus-award-fee arrangement that incorporated the provisions of 48 C.F.R. § 52.216–7 (2000), whereby the Army would reimburse KBR for all costs that it incurred in contract performance, including payments to subcontractors, along with a fee determined by subcontract costs. *See* JX 2, at 7626; Jt. Stipl. I ¶ 9.

Pursuant to the Contract, plaintiff would provide logistics support services, including dining facility ("DFAC") services, to the Army during contingency operations in support of Operation Iraqi Freedom. A "contingency operation" is defined in the Federal Acquisition Regulation ("FAR") as a military operation that

> (1) [i]s designated by the Secretary of Defense as an operation in which members of the armed forces are or may become involved in military actions, operations, or hostilities against an enemy of the United States or against an opposing military force; or
> (2) [r]esults in the call or order to, or retention on, active duty of members of the uniformed services [under specified sections of the United States Code] ... during a war or during a national emergency declared by the President or Congress.

Jt. Stipl. I ¶ 2 (quoting 48 C.F.R. (FAR) § 2.101 (2012)).

The Contract required KBR to provide services to the Army as directed by the issuance of individual task orders ("TOs"). *Id.* ¶ 3. On June 13, 2003, the Army issued to KBR a Notice to Proceed ("NTP") to begin providing logistics services at various locations throughout Iraq, *id.* ¶ 4, involving sites H2 and H4. The Army directed or otherwise prohibited KBR from employing Iraqi or "Host Country" nationals to work in DFACs in connection with the provisioning of DFAC services in Iraq. *Id.* ¶ 6. On August 12, 2003, the Army issued TO 59 to KBR. *Id.* ¶ 7. TO 59 had a period of performance of June 13, 2003, through April 30, 2005—687 days, *id.* ¶ 8—and required KBR to provide, install, operate, and maintain DFACs in accordance with its Statement of Work ("SOW") for permanent and transient camp populations. JX 3, at 12964. The work required was subject to revision through the issuance of a modification to TO 59 or a Letter of Technical ***18** Direction ("LOTD"). Jt. Stipl. I ¶ 10. TO 59 was followed by TO 89, which effectively continued the logistics efforts required under TO 59, including DFAC services at sites H2 and H4. *Id.* ¶ 13. Performance under TO 89 began on May 1, 2005. *Id.* ¶ 12. TO 89 also provided for KBR to be compensated on a cost-plus-award-fee basis and incorporated FAR § 52.216–7. *Id.* ¶ 14.

Plaintiff contracted with subcontractors to provide certain services, such as DFAC services, required by the Army's TOs. Following award of various DFAC subcontracts in the summer of 2003, the Defense Contract Auditing Agency (the "DCAA") expressed concerns regarding the pricing structure of these subcontracts, disagreeing with KBR's use of a fixed, per person/per day ("PPPD") price based on either the headcounts set forth in the subcontracts' SOWs or the number of meals actually served, whichever was higher. *See* Tr. at 910 (plaintiff's counsel); Tr. at 91–92 (Charles A. Carr, KBR's then-Head of the Tiger Team, a DFAC team in charge of administering DFAC subcontracts in Iraq and Kuwait). The DCAA was troubled by the lack of transparency regarding individual cost elements and the fact that KBR was paying its subcontractors for meals that were not served. *See* Tr. at 91–92 (Carr). Additionally, the Army was concerned that it was paying for the DFAC facilities—which were built by the subcontractors and leased by KBR—several times over. *See* Tr. at 94 (Carr).

To address those concerns, KBR, via Mr. Carr, designed a new subcontract structure that KBR used to recompete its DFAC subcontracts in early 2004 when the initial period of performance for the original subcontracts expired. *See* Tr. at 94 (Carr). These second-generation subcontracts contained three 1000–person numerical ranges designated "headcount bands." *See* Tr. at 95 (Carr). Semi-variable and fixed costs were organized into these headcount bands based on the stated capacity that the band encompassed. The middle headcount band was established with reference to the headcount set forth in the subcontracts' SOW. *See* Tr. at 95 (Carr). The upper and lower headcount bands, which were, respectively, 1,000 troops above and 1,000 troops below the range represented by the middle headcount band, were created to account for fluctuations in the number of troops fed. *See* Tr. at 95 (Carr). The upper and lower bands "were both prepriced options that would be implemented with a change order to the subcontractor once [KBR was] directed to change the head count that was contractually required through an LOTD from the client." Tr. at 96 (Carr). This series of subcontracts was referred to as the "SK series." *See id.*

In March 2004 personnel from KBR, DCAA, and the Defense Contract Management Agency ("DCMA") participated in a conference call during which Jill E. Pettibone, a KBR employee who worked with Mr. Carr and the Tiger Team, and Mr. Carr laid out the new subcontract structure. *See* Tr. at 112–16 (Carr). Mr. Carr testified that the conference call participants responded favorably and did not voice any objections to the SK series. *See* Tr. at 116 (Carr). Following the conference call, plaintiff began competing and awarding the SK subcontracts.

<u>The SK 465 Subcontract</u>

SK 465 involved the provision of DFAC services at site H4, which was located near Mosul, Iraq.[2] Mosul, Iraq is located approximately 220 miles north-northwest of Baghdad, Iraq. Jt. Stipl. I ¶ 5. Between July 2003 and March 10, 2004, before implementation of the SK series of subcontracts, DFAC services at site H4, a tent facility, were subcontracted to The Event Source ("TES") under Master Agreement 4 Work Release 7. *Id.* ¶ 30. At the time that plaintiff awarded the initial subcontract to TES, the Army instructed KBR to prepare to serve a camp population of up to 6,196 troops. *See* Def.'s Br. [No. 45] filed Nov. 21, 2011, at 3. In January 2004 KBR issued Request for Proposal No. H4 Mosul DFAC ("RFP") seeking offers for the provisioning of DFAC services at site H4. Jt. Stipl. I ¶ 31. Plaintiff's RFP ***19** initially identified the anticipated headcount at site H4 as 6,196. *Id.* ¶ 32. On February 17, 2004, after KBR issued its RFP but before the submission of bids, Administrative Contracting Officer ("ACO") Russell J. Blaine, having the requisite delegated authority, issued LOTD No. 04–59–CJTF7–03 (the "February 17 LOTD"). JX 6 (Feb. 17, 2004 e-mail from Mr. Blaine to various Army personnel regarding February 17 LOTD

[2] Site H4 previously had been known as "Camp Glory" or "Camp Marez." *See* Def.'s Br. [No. 45] filed Nov. 21, 2011, at 3.

altering anticipated camp populations at five H sites); Jt. Stipl. I ¶ 11. The February 17 LOTD reduced the anticipated camp population at site H4 from 6,196 to 2,573. *See* JX 6. After receiving the February 17 LOTD, KBR amended its RFP to identify the anticipated headcount at site H4 as 2,573. Jt. Stipl. I ¶ 33. KBR instructed offerors that their proposals should set forth pricing for three headcount bands: (1) 1,500–2,500; (2) 2,501–3,500; and (3) 3,501–4,500. JX 7. KBR received six offers in response to its RFP. Jt. Stipl. I ¶ 34.

On March 8, 2004, KBR awarded a subcontract-SK 465–to ABC International Group ("ABC"). Jt. Stipl. I ¶ 35. SK 465 included a SOW with a headcount of 2,573 and had a period of performance of March 8, 2004, through June 12, 2004, with an optional period of performance from June 13, 2004, through June 12, 2005. *Id.* ¶¶ 35–36. ABC was tasked with constructing a Kirby-style (prefabricated metal) DFAC building to replace the existing tent structure as well as the provisioning of DFAC services for a camp population of 2,573. Jt. Stipl. I ¶ 35; *see also* JX 10 (SK 465 as executed by KBR and ABC). ABC's proposed monthly prices for the period beginning June 13, 2004, were, as follows:

SK 465 Monthly Prices Beginning June 13, 2004			
Item/Service	**Price Per**	**Price Per**	**Price Per**
Description	**Headcount**	**Headcount**	**Headcount**
	1,500–2,500	**2,501–3,500**	**3,501–4,500**
Equipment	$ 52,100.00	$ 58,000.00	$ 68,200.00
Refrigeration Units	$ 45,000.00	$ 50,000.00	$ 60,000.00
Generators	$ 31,000.00	$ 31,000.00	$ 31,000.00
Lease of Kirby DFAC	$ 50,000.00	$ 53,735.00	$ 53,735.00
Labor	$395,000.00	$427,000.00	$475,000.00
Consumables	$230,000.00	$250,000.00	$290,000.00

JX 10, at 83026.

Although the award was made on the basis of ABC's being the lowest bidder, that was not the case. *See* Tr. at 163–64 (Carr). Eurest Support Systems ("ESS") priced its proposal $1 million less than ABC's, but, due to a mathematical error in the bid tabulation sheet prepared by Jamal Nasery, KBR DFAC Services, Subcontract Administrator Team Leader, it appeared that ESS's proposal was $100,000.00 more expensive than ABC's. *See* Tr. at 163–64 (Carr); Def.'s Br. [No. 45] filed Nov. 21, 2011, at 4–5. This error, however, was not discovered until after SK 465 had been awarded to ABC. *See* Tr. at 163 (Carr).

Defendant made much of this error, speculating as to projected savings that would have been secured had ESS received the award. For example, Mr. Carr, Mr. Nasery's supervisor, who would not concede that ESS necessarily would have been awarded the SK 465 subcontract based on the error, acknowledged on cross-examination that ESS's long-term costs were over $1 million less than ABC's. *See* Tr. at 163–64 (Carr). Mr. Carr stated that had he discovered Mr. Nasery's error, he "would have sent that [the bid tabulation] back to Jamal and asked him to correct the error, re-evaluate it commercially and make another recommendation."[3] Tr. at 164 (Carr).

***20** On June 7, 2004, Major Thomas D. Hunter, an ACO,[4] issued an LOTD directing KBR to stop the construction of the new Kirby-style DFAC at site H4 ("June 7 LOTD"). Jt. Stipl. I ¶¶ 37–38; *see also* JX 11, at G–0194571 (June 7 LOTD). Major Hunter explained that, out of concern for "force protection," the Army was considering a different site for the DFAC facility. JX 11, at G–0194571. On June 22, 2004, Major Hunter issued LOTD No. 04–59–H4–08 ("June 22 LOTD"). Jt. Stipl. I ¶ 39. The June 22 LOTD provided KBR with notice to proceed to enter into a lease-to-purchase agreement for a new DFAC facility constructed of reinforced concrete in place of the Kirby-style facility provided for in SK 465. *See* JX 12, at G–0194597 (June 22 LOTD). Moreover, the June 22 LOTD increased the SOW base camp population from 2,573 persons to 6,200+ persons. *See id.* It further indicated that KBR should provide the following

---

[3] The court is more concerned with Mr. Nasery's inadequate Price Negotiation Memorandum (the "PNM"), recognized as such long before this case was in litigation. Mr. Carr testified that he determined that Mr. Nasery's analysis was "not adequate because it did not have the level of documentation of support that it would need," Tr. at 172 (Carr), and he agreed that the PNM did not provide a breakdown of the different price components nor how circumstances had or had not changed since the original bid four months earlier. *See* Tr. at 173 (Carr). The problems associated with the PNM are discussed in greater detail *infra*.

[4] Major Hunter has since been promoted to the rank of Lieutenant Colonel. For clarity, however, reference is made herein to "Major Hunter."

information to Major Hunter within five business days:

> a) Estimated cost to perform this effort.
> b) A schedule of activities leading to the successful conclusion of this effort.
> c) Propose[d] performance criteria for government consideration.
> d) Suggested changes to the Statement of Work necessitated by this effort."

Id. At this point, the court finds, plaintiff was responding to exigent circumstances, and Major Hunter's cagey testimony only reinforced the challenge that the Army gave plaintiff.

Thomas R. Donley, then-DFAC Procurement, Material, and Property Manager for Iraq and Kuwait, testified that, upon receipt of the June 22 LOTD, KBR personnel held a meeting to determine what action needed to be taken. *See* Tr. at 195, 233 (Donley). He stated that, although KBR considered issuing a competition for the new work, it ultimately decided to keep ABC on site because

> it was determined because of the [June 7] LOTD, because of the location, because of the sense of urgency ... within which this needed to be dealt with, and because [ABC] was already working to build a DFAC, which is now changing, [KBR] deemed that it was reasonable to keep [ABC] on the site. Also, had [KBR not kept ABC on site], there would have been extensive demobilization costs involved.

Tr. at 233–34 (Donley).

On June 23, 2004, Mr. Nasery requested a proposal for the new work from ABC, which ultimately was embodied in Change Order 1 ("CO 1"). *See* PX 44 (June 23, 2004 e-mail from Mr. Nasery to Waleed Al–Awadi, President & CEO of ABC, requesting proposal in response to June 22 LOTD). ABC submitted its proposal on June 27, 2004. *See* PX 51. The proposal provided prices for three headcount bands. The middle band—5,501 to 6,500 troops—encompassed the increased camp population figure (6,200+) identified in the June 22 LOTD, which would serve as the new SOW headcount. *See* PX 51, at 1399. ABC's proposed monthly prices were, as follows:

ABC's Proposed Monthly Prices for CO			
Item/Service	**Price Per**	**Price Per**	**Price Per**
Description	**Headcount**	**Headcount**	**Headcount**
	4,501–5,500	**5,501–6,500**	**6,501–7,500**
Equipment	$ 145,000.00	$ 145,000.00	$ 174,000.00
Refrigeration Units	$ 125,000.00	$ 125,000.00	$ 149,000.00
Generators	$ 177,500.00	$ 177,500.00	$ 194,200.00
DFAC Concrete Building	$ 566,000.00	$ 566,000.00	$ 598,200.00
Labor	$1,067,500.00	$1,067,500.00	$1,188,600.00
Consumables	$ 528,000.00	$ 625,000.00	$ 721,000.00

***21** PX 58, at 0609.

ABC also proposed plans and specifications for the new DFAC, which would be constructed with reinforced concrete and would include a VIP dining room.[5] *See* PX 51, at 1400. ABC explained that its proposed rates were based on a twelve-month amortization period ending on June 12, 2005, and after which time KBR would receive ownership of the facility, refrigeration units ("reefers"[6]), and generators. *Id.* at 1397. The monthly cost for the new capacity was $2,606,000.00—almost triple the cost of SK 465 as initially awarded. ABC provided a follow-up to its proposal submission in an unsolicited e-mail "clarify[ing] the prices offered to serve 6200 persons." PX 49 (June 27, 2004 e-mail from Mr. Al–Awadi to

[5] The parties disagree about whether the Army requested the VIP room. Major Hunter testified that he did not direct KBR to include such a room, *see* Tr. at 435–36. (Hunter), but a February 26, 2004 LOTD from Major Hunter's predecessor, Major Ramona McCaa, states that "[t]he Government requests KBR to install a VIP meeting room inside the DFAC located on H4. This room will accommodate any VIP luncheons and meetings," *see* PX 84, at 0562. The court finds that the VIP room was an included requirement.

[6] According to Mr. Donley, a reefer is a mobile refrigerated containerized unit, or semi-truck with a refrigerator unit. Tr. at 315 (Donley).

Mr. Nasery regarding the prices in ABC's June 27, 2004 proposal). Mr. Al–Awadi's e-mail explained that, in order to serve the increased camp population, additional generators, freezers, kitchen and serving equipment, and dining hall furniture would be needed, as well as "a minimum of 240 personnel." *Id.* Citing the "current violence and the beheading of hostages by terrorists," Mr. Al–Awadi noted "a drastic increase in the cost of labor and a severe shortage of available staff who are willing to work in Iraq." *Id.* According to ABC, these factors accounted for the cost of its new proposal.

On June 28, 2004, Mr. Nasery forwarded ABC's proposal to Philip Parenti, a consultant to KBR with an expertise in DFACs and camp catering, *see* Tr. at 312 (Donley), for further review. *See* PX 51, at 1397. On July 5, 2004, ABC, at KBR's request, furnished additional information regarding its proposal to Mr. Nasery. *See* PX 53 (July 5, 2004 e-mail from Mr. Al–Awadi to Mr. Nasery providing information clarifying its proposal). Mr. Al–Awadi again commented on the increased cost of labor resulting from the violence-induced labor shortage. *See id.* at 0188–89 ("This increased cost of labor...includes salaries, benefits, indemnity, bonuses, medical examinations, insurance, air tickets from home countries to Kuwait, and [additional transportation costs resulting from] unsafe passage by road from Kuwait to Mosul.").

On July 10, 2004, Messrs. Parenti, Nasery, and Al–Awadi, along with Terry Kleinsasser, a KBR Subcontract Administrator, met to discuss ABC's proposal. *See* DX 103, at 0924–25 (draft of memorandum summarizing discussions at July 10, 2004 meeting regarding ABC's proposal). The attendees discussed the need to add and remove various pieces of equipment, and KBR representatives opined that labor costs were 10% too high. *See id.* at 0924. Despite the airing of these issues, the record contains no evidence indicating that ABC modified its proposal in any way following the meeting. *See* Def.'s Br. filed June 8, 2012, at 9–10 [No. 09–428C]; Pl's Br. filed May 25, 2012, at 25 [No. 09–428C]. On July 16, 2004, Mr. Nasery authored a Price Negotiation Memorandum (the "PNM"), which concluded that ABC's proposed prices were reasonable. *See* PX 58, at 0612–13 (CO 1 containing Mr. Nasery's PNM). Mr. Nasery's PNM, however, was based on an analytic flaw that was not discovered until later. In justifying ABC's prices, Mr. Nasery stated that

> [s]ince the U.S. Army has doubled the headcount at [site H4] and therefore stopped construction to redesign[ ] a larger ***22** upgraded DFAC [that will be] double the size thus doubling the necessary equipment and labor as well, it is decided to justify the new revised rates by a comparable analysis by doubling the originally competed rates on [SK 465].

PX 58, at 0612. Essentially, Mr. Nasery's methodology justified a quadrupling of the total price because he doubled not only the number of troops to be served, multiplied by the rate per person, but also the per-person rate. Mr. Nasery's task was to justify the price given the exigencies of war. Those circumstances did not justify the inadequacy that his memorandum displayed in this respect, as well as others.[7]

Prior to its execution, proposed CO 1 was subject to KBR's greensheet-approval process, which is "the approval authorization trail ... for any type of transaction or subcontractor contract that KBR made." Tr. at 331 (Donley). The greensheet-approval process was a review of the actions taken "in the field" by Mr. Nasery and others regarding proposed CO 1. *See* Def.'s Br. filed June 8, 2012, at 11 [No. 09–428C]. Mr. Donley testified that he, along with Mr. Parenti; Mr. Nasery; Tom Quigley, Procurement, Material, and Property Manager for Iraq; and Wayne Agness, KBR Food Service Project Manager, undertook a technical review and analysis of all documents supporting CO 1 to determine if CO 1 should be approved and implemented. *See* Tr. at 332–34, 374–75 (Donley). He stated that

> the team ... would have thoroughly reviewed all the required documents, and the packet [of CO 1 documents] that would have been delivered to me would have been complete, and I would have made sure that all the attachments referred to were in place. I would have read through everything ... and what it ... discussed in writing to make sure, and I was satisfied that it covered, even in many different ways, what was desired by the [Army].

[7] *See* note 3 *supra.*

....

> I knew exactly what to expect [in CO 1] because it was something that had been thoroughly discussed amongst ourselves in the analyzation of it and the procedures that we needed to follow to implement it.

Tr. at 332–34 (Donley). According to Mr. Donley, his analysis of CO 1 as part of the greensheet-approval process included review of Mr. Nasery's PNM to ensure that it sufficiently justified the expenditure. *See* Tr. at 334 (Donley). Following this review, on July 17, 2004, CO 1 received greensheet approval, having been approved by Messrs. Nasery, Donley, and Quigley. *See* PX 58, at 0611. CO 1 was executed by KBR and ABC on the same day. *See* PX 58, at 608–10; Jt. Stipl. I ¶ 41.

Mr. Donley impressed the court with his percipient knowledge of the situation on the ground at the time. He was a sincere and earnest witness who credibly characterized plaintiff's timely delivery of the June 7 and June 22 LOTD requirements with the statement "I would humbly submit that [it] would be quite an achievement stateside in any city let alone in a war zone." Tr. at 324–25 (Donley). Nonetheless, defendant on cross-examination was able to distance Mr. Donley from his general overall endorsement of Mr. Nasery's PNM. Mr. Donley conceded that the PNM "lacked lots of details that in hindsight should have been included and they weren't there." Tr. at 377 (Donley).

> BY MR. PROUTY:
>
> Q Now do you consider this a reasonable way to justify the prices of a change order?
>
> A I would say that I would do it differently today.
>
> Q And again that's not the question. Now is that a reasonable way of calculating the reasonableness of the prices of the change order?
>
> A I don't know.

Q This document does not discuss facility costs, does it?

A Not specifically.

Q Nor any individual price components, correct?

A Correct.

Q Although it refers to the prevailing conditions and circumstances at the bottom ***23** of the page, it does not describe how they have changed, does it?

A Say again sir.

Q I'm sorry?

A Could you repeat that, please.

Q Certainly. Although it says it's fair and reasonable for the type of work required under the prevailing conditions and circumstances, it does not set forth how those prevailing conditions and circumstances might have changed since the originally competed subcontract, does it?

A No, it's not detailed there, not at all.

Tr. at 367–69 (Donley).[8]

Pursuant to CO 1, ABC was to recover its costs to perform DFAC services through twelve monthly payments, at the end of which time KBR would own—on the Army's behalf—the new concrete DFAC, as well as all reefers and generators. To enable the twelve monthly payments, CO 1 was made retroactive to June 13, 2004—the beginning of SK 465's option period. Jt. Stipl. I ¶ 42; Pl.'s Br. filed Oct. 31, 2011, at 23.

---

[8] The court agrees with plaintiff that defendant may be pressing the point by criticizing Mr. Nasery's PNM for not addressing economics of scale. However, the PNM's other omissions were significant.

Shortly after CO 1 was executed by KBR and ABC, ACO Major Hunter requested documentation revealing the "delta cost increase from the original DFAC to the new designed and larger DFAC at H4." PX 63, at 1377–78 (June 27 to August 2, 2004 e-mail chain among Army, KBR, and ABC personnel); *see also* PX 64, at 1863–64 (same). In response Mr. Nasery provided two tables that depicted total annual costs for SK 465 and CO 1. *See* PX 63, at 1381. The tables indicated that the "Grand Total for the original DFAC" was $13,767,635.71, and the "Grand total for the new DFAC" was $33,870,666.00. *See id.* Despite the quoted titles, the stated dollar amounts included costs for all items and services for which ABC was responsible, not solely the facility costs. *See* PX 70, at 0221. Major Hunter mistakenly concluded that the $33–million figure was the total price for only the new DFAC facility. *See id.* at 0222. On September 8, 2004, he e-mailed Mr. Nasery, expressing concern that construction of the DFAC appeared to be a "massive undertaking" costing $33 million. *See id.* at 0221–22. In accordance with KBR policy, Gordon Wohlfeil, KBR Project Manager for Northern Iraq, responded to Major Hunter's concerns. *See* PX 71. Mr. Wohlfeil clarified that the $33–million figure—which actually was $37 million—was "inclusive of all facilities, labor, and consumables" and that "[t]he lease purchase of the DFAC by itself [was] $7,738,726 if you include new mobilization costs." *See id.* at 4826. He further stated that the $33–million (or $37–million) cost assumed a headcount of 6,200 but noted that "[w]e've yet to break 2500 in headcount." *Id.* When Major Hunter responded with surprise that the headcount had not exceeded 2,500 troops, Mr. Wohlfeil informed him that, although he would look into it, "the headcount for yesterday was less than 2,000." *See id.* at 4825.

Given that Major Hunter's June 22 LOTD also functioned as a NTP, once KBR and ABC executed CO 1, ABC began to perform pursuant to it. *See* Tr. at 400–02 (Hunter). Major Hunter apparently accepted Mr. Wohlfeil's explanation, *see* Tr. at 409–10 (Hunter), because he raised no further objections and did not order KBR to stop work. *See* Pl.'s Br. filed June 22, 2012, at 8. Nor did he issue a subsequent LOTD modifying the SOW anticipated capacity upon learning that actual headcounts were not even approaching the 6,200+ SOW figure—an action that he had authority to take. *See* Tr. at 391–92 (Hunter). Indeed, the Army and Major Hunter were less responsive to the realities on the ground than plaintiff was responsive to the LOTDs.

On April 29, 2005, the Army commenced TO 89 by issuing a limited NTP. TO 89 continued TO 59 at site H4 and anticipated a camp population of 6,200 or more. Jt. Stipl. I ¶ 13. Performance under TO 89 began on May 1, 2005. *Id.* ¶ 12. KBR paid ABC in accordance with the terms of SK 465 and CO 1. KBR included amounts paid to ABC in vouchers submitted to the Army for reimbursement in accordance with TOs 59 and 89. The Army paid KBR's vouchers. On June ***24** 12, 2005, the date on which performance of SK 465 ended, title to the reinforced concrete DFAC at site H4 passed to the Army. *Id.* ¶ 44. As of June 9, 2011, the Army was continuing to use the DFAC. *Id.* ¶ 43.

In July 2007 KBR personnel became aware that DCAA was reviewing KBR's justification for the costs associated with construction of the concrete DFAC at site H4. *See* DX 90, at 3783–84. Borbala "Bori" Ungvari, a Subcontract Administrator in KBR's Procurement Compliance Department, stated in an e-mail to Greg Whitty, KBR's Senior Manager, Project Controls, that "[t]he file doesn't have adequate price justification so we are trying to find historical data that we can use for the basis of comparison to justify the price after the fact." *Id.* at 3783. KBR personnel exchanged various information via e-mail regarding pricing. *See id.* at 3770–84. On July 24, 2007, Mr. Carr e-mailed Craig Castellana, KBR's then-Procurement Supply Manager for LOGCAP III, instructing him to review SK 465 and draft a price-reasonableness justification. *See* Tr. at 460–61 (Castellana); DX 90, at 3770. Mr. Carr explained that, because Mr. Nasery's PNM was not adequate, it was necessary that someone prepare a new price-fair-and-reasonableness determination for CO 1 to SK 465. *See* DX 90, at 3770. Upon receiving Mr. Carr's e-mail, Mr. Castellana, along with his supervisor, George Nguyen, called Mr. Carr, who requested the new justification "in short order." Tr. at 462 (Castellana). Mr. Castellana testified that he was directed to "go back and look at the contract file and review the original price justification, and look specifically at the building itself, and ... write an updated price justification based on the facility." Tr. at 460–61 (Castellana).

Mr. Carr also instructed Mr. Whitty and Jorge Alberch, a Senior Estimator, KBR Estimating, to prepare an Independent Cost Estimate ("ICE") for the H4 DFAC. *See* DX 90, at 3770–80. Mr. Carr selected Messrs. Whitty and Alberch to perform the ICE because they had experience building facilities in Iraq and Afghanistan. *See* Tr. at 176 (Carr). The ICE would use KBR's internal analysis to compare the H4 DFAC to other, similar DFACs and thereby determine a reasonable price for the H4 DFAC in CO 1. *See* Tr. at 180 (Carr). However, Messrs. Whitty and Alberch both were included in the e-mail chain initiated by Ms. Ungvari announcing the need for an adequate price justification of the H4 DFAC price in CO 1. *See* DX 90. They therefore were aware that the total purchase price for the H4 DFAC was approximately $7 million and had a target in mind when they set out to perform what was deemed an independent analysis. *See* Tr. at 177–78 (Carr); DX 90, at 3779, 3783.

Paul A. Christianson, Project Manager of KBR's Design and Construction Group, provided Messrs. Whitty and Alberch with a DFAC to use in performing the ICE. *See* DX 90, at 3781–82. The building—Q-West—was located in Jordan, but Mr. Carr mistakenly testified that it was located in Mosul in northern Iraq. *See* Tr. at 181 (Carr), 1642, 1644–45, 1648 (Check). Q–West measured out at approximately 3,400 square meters. *See* Tr. at 179 (Carr). H4, however, was approximately 5,000 square meters. *See* DX 90, at 3783; Tr. at 180 (Carr). To enable a more meaningful comparison, Messrs. Whitty and Alberch applied an area adjustment to Q–West, which effectively rendered it 4,500 square meters for comparison purposes. *See* JX 27, at 0422; Tr. at 182–83 (Carr). Messrs. Whitty and Alberch e-mailed the finished ICE to Mr. Carr on July 23, 2007. *See* DX 90, at 3772. The ICE indicated a cost of $6,781,224.00 for the H4 DFAC, including mechanical, plumbing, and electrical costs. *See* JX 27, at 422; Tr. at 184 (Carr).

Thereafter, Messrs. Castellana and Nguyen began their assignment to prepare an adequate price justification for the cost of the H4 DFAC in CO 1. They adopted a two-pronged approach, which utilized the ICE and a second facility for comparison purposes, *see* Tr. at 184 (Carr), after reviewing KBR's fifty-one subcontracts in order to identify a second facility that was similar in size—in terms of headcount—to the concrete DFAC at site H4 that could be used as a comparable, *see* Tr. at 462–63 (Castellana). Because KBR procurement guidelines provided that, when performing a comparative price analysis, employees should use for comparison***25** items that are no greater than one year old at the time of the analysis, Messrs. Castellana and Nguyen selected the dining facility at site D 16 at Camp Kalsu in south-central Iraq. *See* Tr. at 463–64, 469 (Castellana). The D 16 facility had been built recently and had a SOW headcount of 5,050 troops, plus a twenty-percent surge, yielding a total headcount of 6,060. *See* Tr. at 463–65 (Castellana). Other DFACs with similar SOW headcounts existed, but Mr. Castellana explained that he chose the DFAC at site D 16 because it offered the most current pricing.[9] *See* Tr. at 464–65 (Castellana).

Although the D16 DFAC was intended to serve a similar SOW headcount as the H4 DFAC, the two facilities had considerable differences. The D 16 DFAC was a Kirby-style—i.e., prefabricated—structure with "soft-skinned" aluminum walls that lacked built-in force protection. *See* Tr. at 467 (Castellana). The H4 DFAC, on the other hand, had built-in force protection in that the walls, flooring, and ceiling were reinforced concrete. *See* Tr. at 467 (Castellana). To account for those differences, Mr. Castellana added the cost of concrete T-walls[10] that could surround the D 16 facility in order to offer comparable force protection to the actual cost of the D 16 DFAC. *See* Tr. at 467–68 (Castellana). He did not, however, factor in a cost for overhead protective structures. *See* Tr. at 473 (Castellana). Mr. Castellana attested that the level of violence at the H4 DFAC was comparable to that experienced at the D 16 DFAC. *See* Tr. at 469–70 (Castellana).

Messrs. Castellana and Nguyen's undertaking culminated in a two-page memorandum authored by Mr. Castellana on July 26, 2007 (the "2007 Justification"). *See* Tr. at 473 (Castellana); JX 26. The 2007 Justification was accompanied by three attachments. *See* JX 27. The first attachment contained documents that Mr. Al–Awadi had sent to Mr. Nasery in June 2004 when Mr. Nasery was preparing to draft his PNM for CO 1. Included were a sketch of the layout for the H4 DFAC, a list of materials that ABC intended to use to construct the DFAC, and the anticipated monthly costs for three headcount bands. *See id.* at 0399–0403. The second attachment contained the pricing schedule for the D16 DFAC. *See id.* at 0405–08. Finally, KBR's ICE was included as the third attachment. *See id.* at 0410–22.

[9] It is not clear to the court why a facility with the most current pricing would be the best comparable by which to assess the reasonableness of the costs associated with a facility constructed several years earlier. The court sought clarification of this logic from Mr. Castellana, who stated that that was the policy and he followed it. *See* Tr. at 464–67 (Castellana).

[10] T-walls are concrete blocks placed around the perimeter of a permanent or temporary structure. Tr. at 468 (Castellana). The T-walls depicted at trial were twelve feet tall, six feet wide, and weighed approximately 64,000 pounds each. Tr. at 468 (Castellana); *see* PX 187. They "provide blast protection from rockets and mortars and small arms fire to an otherwise unprotected building." Tr. at 468 (Castellana).

In concluding the 2007 Justification, Mr. Castellana stated that "[t]he pricing that was paid for the building at H 4 under subcontract SK 00465 is fair and reasonable based on a comparable procurement with the additional protective measures added and KBR's independent cost estimates of the DFAC facility construction." JX 26, at 0393. Presumably, the 2007 Justification was sent to DCAA, which performed an audit of KBR's incurred costs on SK 465.

On November 28, 2007, DCAA issued a Notice of Contract Costs Suspended and/or Disapproved (the "Original Form 1") suspending payment of certain costs that KBR paid to ABC pursuant to CO 1 such as costs for dining equipment, the facility lease, reefers, generators, labor, and consumables, and totaled $11,337,261.00. JX 29. DCAA supplemented the Original Form 1 on December 12, 2008. *See* JX 36, at G–0027597 (discussing December 12, 2008 exit conference). It subsequently issued a revised Notice of Contract Costs Suspended and/or Disapproved (the "Revised Form 1") on July 8, 2009, disapproving $12,529,504.00 of KBR's costs incurred in paying ABC pursuant to CO 1. *See* JX 36, at G–0027590 (DCAA Revised Form 1, dated July 1, 2009 and received by KBR's Accounting Supervisor on July 8, 2009); Jt. Stipl. I ¶ 45. The Revised Form 1 provided, as follows:

***26** We are disapproving $12,529,504 relating to dining facilities (DFAC) subcontract costs billed under LOGCAP III Contract No. DAAA09–02–D–0007 for ABC International Corporation subcontract SK00465 as unreasonable pursuant to FAR 31.201–3, Determining Reasonableness. We consider the costs as unreasonable because KBR[ ] performed an inadequate analysis related to (i) the prices for higher headcount bands, and (ii) the costs of building a new DFAC facility. In addition, KBR[ ] billed costs using a headband that was significantly higher than the actual headcount served.

JX 36, at G–0027590. The Revised Form 1 differed from the previous version not only in amount but also in that it no longer questioned the amounts that KBR paid to ABC for reefers and generators. On October 1, 2008, KBR filed a certified claim challenging the Government's withholding of the amount disapproved in the Revised Form 1 regarding SK 465 and CO 1. Joint Stipulation filed Mar. 28, 2012, ¶ 1 ("Jt. Stipl. II"). The claim was received by the Government on October 6, 2008. *Id.*

The parties each presented experts to opine on the reasonableness of KBR's incurred costs from ABC. James J. Check, Managing Director, Chess Consulting LLC, qualified as plaintiff's expert on the subjects of government contract cost and pricing and the application of the FAR to government contracts. *See* Tr. at 818–19 (court). Mr. Check performed a price analysis[11] of the prices agreed to by KBR in CO 1. Tr. at 822–23 (Check); *see also* PX 142, at 10–11 (Mr. Check's expert report for No. 09–428C regarding SK 465 and CO 1). He testified that price analysis—as compared to cost analysis—is the preferred method of determining reasonableness under the FAR, particularly when the technique utilized to execute a price analysis is price competition or comparison to previously approved prices. *See* Tr. at 823 (Check).

To assess the reasonableness of the prices in CO 1, Mr. Check's price analysis compared the prices in CO 1 with the prices in SK 465, which had been obtained by way of a price competition among various bidders. *See* Tr. at 824 (Check). He prepared the following chart to depict his analysis:

Original Subcontract			***CO 1***		
Description	**[1] Price Per**	**[2] Price Per**	**[3] Price Per**	**[4] Price Per**	**[5]% Change**
	the Aug.	**Person**	**the Aug.**	**Person**	**(2,573 vs.**
	Head count of	**(Head count of**	**Head count of**	**(Head count of**	**6,200+**
	2,501–3,500	**2,573)**	**5,501–6,500**	**6,200+)**	**Headcount)**
	per day		**per day**		
Equipment	$58,000	$22.54	$145,000	$23.39	3.75%
Labor	427,000	165.95	1,067,500	172.18	3.75%
Consumables	250,000	97.16	625,000	100.81	3.75%
Totals	$735,000	$285.66	$1,837,500	$296.37	3.75%

[11] A price analysis is "the evaluation of a contract price without looking at the individual cost elements or profit that make up that price." Tr. at 822 (Check).

See PX 142, at 11. Explaining the process underlying his analysis, Mr. Check testified, as follows:

[O]n the left you'll see a column headed original subcontract, so that's of course the SK465 original subcontract pricing. And listed there [in the column marked No. 1] is the price per month of the middle band for [equipment, labor, and consumables]. And then [as depicted in the column marked No. 2] I took the statement of work target headcount for the original subcontract of 2573 and came up with a price per person per month based on that target headcount.

Moving to the right, I did the same thing with CO1 in that I took the middle band pricing figure [as seen in the column marked No. 3], used the statement of work target headcount of 6200 and came up with a price per person per month [depicted in the column marked No. 4].

And then the far right column [column No. 5] shows the percentage change between***27** the two price per persons at the target statement of work headcount figures [column Nos. 2 and 4], and ... it shows a 3.75 percent increase in Change Order 1.

Tr. at 824 (Check). When asked why he used SK 465's middle headcount band—2,501–3,500 persons—Mr. Check responded that he wanted to determine a per-person price for the SOW headcount figure (2,573), which fell within the middle headcount band and thus was subject to the pricing listed therein. *See* Tr. at 825 (Check). Accordingly, he followed the same process to determine a per-person price for the SOW headcount figure in CO 1, which was 6,200 persons. *See* Tr. at 825–26 (Check). Mr. Check concluded that a 3.75% increase was "a very modest increase[,] ... akin to an inflation adjustment that you often see with the passage of some time." Tr. at 826 (Check). Seemingly conceding that a significant amount of time had not passed between execution of SK 465 and CO 1, Mr. Check remarked that the increasing violence and difficulty obtaining laborers accounted for the percentage increase. *See* Tr. at 826–27 (Check). The CO 1 prices, he concluded, thus were reasonable. *See* Tr. at 836 (Check).

Mr. Check also analyzed the price KBR paid for construction of the reinforced concrete DFAC at site H4. *See* Tr. at 829 (Check). For comparison Mr. Check opted to use the DFAC at site D16. *See* PX 142, at 10–11. Mr. Check recognized that, unlike the concrete H4 facility, the D16 DFAC was a Kirby-style facility that lacked overhead protection.[12] *See* Tr. at 829–30 (Check). However, he emphasized that the price of the D16 DFAC was considered reasonable because it was obtained based on adequate price competition and that the anticipated headcount was in line with that for the H4 facility. Tr. at 829–30, 839 (Check). To compare the DFACs, Mr. Check computed a price per person by dividing the total price of each facility by the headcount provided in the SOW for that facility. *See* PX 142, at 10. The result can be illustrated, as follows:

	H4	**D16**
Price	$6,792,000.00	$6,474,500.00
Headcount	6,200+	5,050
Price Per Person	$1,095.48	$1,282.08

See PX 142, at 10. Based on his comparison of the price per person for each facility, Mr. Check concluded that the H4 price was reasonable. *See* Tr. at 830–31 (Check). He explained that "the H4 number is lower and that's indicative of a reasonable price, particularly when one considers that the D–16 number does not include overhead protection, which I've learned ... [is] in the neighborhood of[,] if you price it out[,] $10 or $11 million." Tr. at 830 (Check).

Sandra A. ("Sam") Hadley, Partner, Cotton & Company LLP, qualified as defendant's expert on the subjects of auditing and accounting in relation to government contracts, price reasonableness determinations, and the application of the FAR to government contracts. *See* Tr. at 1190 (court). Ms. Hadley began her testimony by noting that, although SK 465 was awarded to ABC pursuant to a price competition, the award resulted from a flawed bid tabulation, which, if performed correctly, would have shown that ESS, not ABC, was the low bidder. *See* Tr. at 1203–05 (Hadley); *see also* Tr. at 163–64 (Carr); Def.'s Br. [No. 45] filed Nov. 21, 2011, at 4–5. Indeed,

[12] The D 16 DFAC actually lacked side protection, as well as overhead protection; however, the facility price that Mr. Check used for comparison was that determined by Mr. Castellana when he prepared the 2007 Justification and thus included the cost of T-wall side protection to render the D 16 facility more similar to the H4 one.

ESS's bid was approximately $1 million less than ABC's. *See* Tr. at 1204 (Hadley). Ms. Hadley thus challenged Mr. Check's emphasis on the fact that he was comparing CO 1 prices to the competitively awarded prices in SK 465, explaining that ***28** "we don't know had ESS been awarded [SK 465] what they would have proposed for Change Order 1 prices." Tr. at 1205 (Hadley). As stated above, the court views this criticism as too conjectural, as the projected cost impact of this discrepancy cannot be determined.

Ms. Hadley next questioned KBR's ability to evaluate the reasonableness of the prices, given that the prices in SK 465 and CO 1 commingled the costs of constructing a Kirby-style facility and a concrete DFAC, respectively, with the other costs to administer the contract, such as labor and consumables, rendering it difficult to determine to what extent the unit prices apart from the facility's cost would have remained constant. *See* Tr. at 1208–09 (Hadley). Despite this inherent difficulty, Ms. Hadley noted that KBR undertook to perform various reasonableness assessments. She criticized Mr. Nasery's PNM for its "flawed methodology," Tr. at 1207 (Hadley), which "assumed that the unit price would double," Tr. at 1211 (Hadley). According to Ms. Hadley, it was more likely that, as capacity increased, "the unit price would either stay the same or decline with economies of scale." Tr. at 1213 (Hadley). Although Ms. Hadley's objection to doubling of the price is reasonable, the court does not fault plaintiff's price justification analysis on the specific ground that it failed to take account of economies of scale. Ms. Hadley's analysis of Mr. Check's approach to his headband in all other respects was apt.

Regarding the 2007 Justification prepared by Mr. Castellana, Ms. Hadley opined that "the analysis done by comparing the H4 building price in the change order to the two other buildings [the D 16 and Q–West facilities] that were selected [was] inadequate to support the reasonableness of the price for the H4 building" because D16 was not of the same construction as the H4 DFAC and both D16 and Q–West were smaller in size and built in a different time frame. Tr. at 1216–17 (Hadley). Despite testimony that the D16 facility had a similar headcount as the H4 DFAC, Ms. Hadley stated: "I don't believe that it's comparable.... I believe that the size of the building and the type of construction have a much more significant impact on the reasonableness of the price than a head count capacity would." Tr. at 1217 (Hadley). Finally, as for the ICE, Ms. Hadley expressed the opinion that it was not a truly independent estimate because it was prepared after the fact by individuals who knew the price that was being justified. *See* Tr. at 1221–22 (Hadley). She ultimately concluded that "KBR did not [e]nsure [that] the DFAC [b]uilding [p]rice was [r]easonable." DX 91, at 10.

Ms. Hadley submitted a report that set forth textually and graphically her separate conclusion that KBR had failed to justify the component prices in CO 1. *See* DX 91 (Ms. Hadley's expert report for No. 09–428C regarding SK 465 and CO 1). Unlike Mr. Check's analysis, Ms. Hadley's analysis used the monthly price for each headcount band since only one price was proposed for all headcounts that fell within a given headcount band. *See id.* at 11; Tr. at 1233 (Hadley). Ms. Hadley prepared the bar graph reproduced below to depict the price increase for each element from SK 465 to CO 1. *See* DX 91, at 11. The first three numbers on the bottom of the bar graph—2000, 3000, and 4000—represent the medians of the headcount bands from SK 465, while the latter three numbers are the medians of the headcount bands in CO 1. *See id.* The numbers on the left side depict the range of monthly prices for each element.

Monthly Price (Excluding Facility Price) By Headcount Band

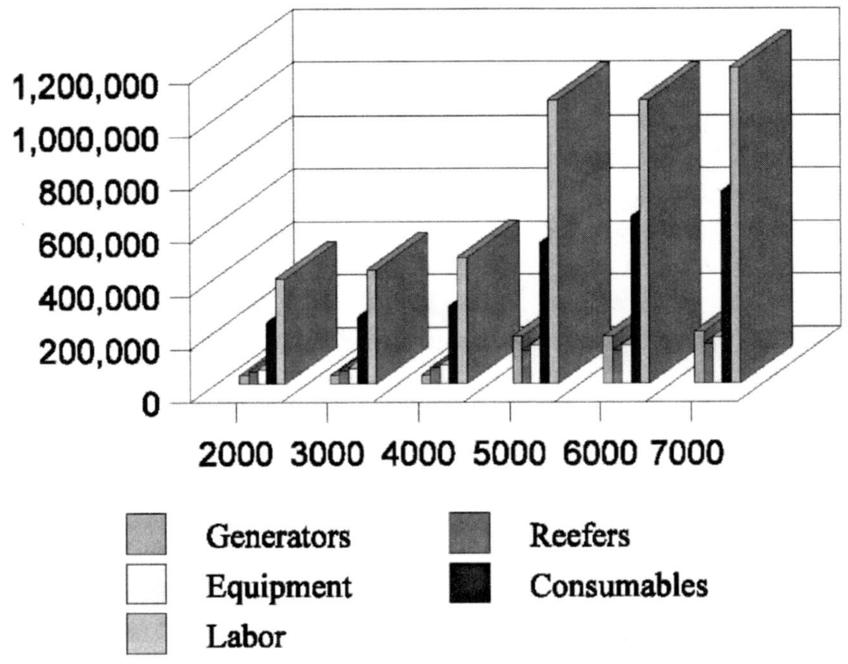

***29** *Id.* Ms. Hadley explained that, as evidenced by the bar graph,

> [e]very price element shows a significant increase from the original, competitive subcontract pricing to the non-competitive pricing in Change Order 1. As a whole (excluding the dining facility) the price more than doubled from the 4,000 count headband [the high headcount band] in the original subcontract to the 5,000 headcount band [the low headcount band] in Change Order 1.

Id. In light of the sizable price increases, Ms. Hadley stated that, had the PNM not been based on a flawed methodology, it would have led KBR to question ABC's proposed prices for CO 1, and it would have been unlikely that management would have approved the prices. *See id.* Accordingly, Ms. Hadley concluded that "KBR [i]gnored [a]vailable [d]ocumentation [i]ndicating that [p]roposed [c]ost [c]omponent [p]ricing was [u]nreasonable." *Id.*

<u>The SK 466 Subcontract</u>

SK 466 involved the provision of DFAC services at site H2, which was located near Mosul, Iraq. There is no contention that the prices agreed upon in SK 466 and Change Order 7 to SK 466 ("CO 7") were not reasonable; rather, the issue presented is whether KBR paid its subcontractor, ABC, in accordance with the terms of SK 466 and CO 7. Between July 2003 and March 10, 2004, before implementation of the SK series of subcontracts, DFAC services at site H2, as with those at site H4, were subcontracted to TES under Master Agreement 4 Work Release 5. Jt. Stipl. I ¶ 15. In January 2004 KBR issued a RFP seeking offers for the provisioning of DFAC services at site H2. *Id.* ¶ 16. KBR's RFP initially identified the anticipated headcount at site H2 as 6,252. *Id.* ¶ 17. After KBR received the February 17 LOTD, which reduced the anticipated camp population at site H2 from 6,252 to 2,929, KBR modified its RFP to reflect the new anticipated headcount. *Id.* ¶ 18; *see also* JX 6. KBR received five offers in response to its RFP. Jt. Stipl. I ¶ 19. In March 2004 KBR awarded a subcontract—SK466—to ABC for the provisioning of DFAC services at site H2. *Id.* ¶ 20; *see also* PX 185, at 6577–78. SK 466 included a SOW with a headcount of 2,929 and had a period of performance from March 11, 2004, through June 12, 2004, with an optional period of performance from June 13, 2004, through June 12, 2005. Jt. Stipl. I ¶¶ 20–21. Like SK 465, SK 466 utilized a headcount band structure pursuant to which KBR would pay ABC.

For some months in 2004, actual headcount at site H2 was lower than that represented ***30** by the middle headcount band, which was created based on the SOW headcount. *See* Def.'s Br. filed June 8, 2012, at 1 [No. 09–578C]; Pl.'s Br. filed Oct. 31, 2011, at 2 [No. 09–578C]. In January 2005 the monthly Maximum Average Daily ("MAD")[13] headcount at site H2 exceeded 4,500. Jt. Stipl. I ¶ 22. The monthly MAD headcount also exceeded 4,500 in March and April 2005. *Id.* ¶ 23. Despite the magnitude of this surge, ABC fed the additional troops. The headcount bands in SK 466 for the optional period within which ABC was operating when the surge occurred were, as follows:

SK 466 Headcount Bands for Optional Period June 13, 2004–June 12, 2005			
June 13, 2004–June 12, 2005			
Item/Service	**Price Per**	**Price Per**	**Price Per**
Description	**Month**	**Month**	**Month**
	1,501–2,500	**2,501–3,500**	**3,501–4,500**
Equipment	$ 16,100.00	$ 16,100.00	$ 16,100.00
Reefers	$ 7,900.00	$ 7,900.00	$ 7,900.00
Generators	$ 5,200.00	$ 5,200.00	$ 5,200.00
Lease of Kirby DFAC	$ 10,800.00	$ 10,800.00	$ 10,800.00
Labor	$558,130.00	$583,200.00	$698,500.00
Consumables	$267,300.00	$298,400.00	$445,100.00

See JX 34, at 9129 (Plaintiff's December 19, 2008 Contract Disputes Act Claim). Accordingly, when the headcount at site H2 exceeded 4,500 beginning in January 2005, there was no pricing structure that accounted for the surge.

[13] KBR explains that, "[t]o calculate the MAD headcount, KBR first determines the highest headcount at any one meal during a day for each day during a month. The mean of these daily headcounts is the MAD." Pl.'s Br. filed Oct. 31, 2011, at 16 n. 9 [No. 09–578C].

To compensate ABC for providing meals in excess of the SOW headcount, KBR and ABC entered negotiations for CO 7. ABC proposed adding a new headcount band for 4,501–5,500 troops in order to provide a pricing structure for the additional capacity. Jt. Stipl. I ¶ 25. The proposed pricing for the new headcount band was, as follows:

Headcount Band Added by CO 7	
Item/Service Description	**Price Per Month 4,501–5,500**
Equipment	$ 28,600.00
Reefers (and Dry–Storage Units)	$ 14,200.00
Generators	$ 9,500.00
Lease	$ 10,800.00
Labor	$863,200.00
Consumables	$556,375.00

See JX 21, at G–0173882–83 (CO 7). KBR agreed to the prices in the new headcount band on February 25, 2005. *See* JX 19, at 2257–58. Despite having reached an agreement, the parties did not execute CO 7 until June 14, 2005. Jt. Stipl. I ¶ 24. CO 7, however, was effective retroactive to January 1, 2005. *See* Tr. at 1611 (Paula J. "Penny" Battles, Procurement Supply Manager for LOGCAP III); JX 21, at G–0173882.

Ms. Battles testified that, based solely on its terms, CO 7 called for payment to ABC ***31** according to the headcount band in which monthly headcounts fell. *See* Tr. at 1611 (Battles). Note 8 to CO 7 provides that "[f]or other [non-SOW] headcount prices, refer to Tables 2, 3 & 4," PX 185, at 6454, suggesting that variable price components were to be paid in accordance with the actual monthly headcount. The parties disagree as to CO 7's payment terms.

On January 15, 2008, DCAA issued a Form 1, suspending $783,342.00 of KBR's direct costs, indirect costs, and fee. *See* Jt. Stipl. I ¶ 27; JX 30, at G–0602875–91 (DCAA Original Form 1 regarding SK 466 and CO 7, dated January 15, 2008). KBR remitted the total suspended amount to the United States Treasury by check dated May 22, 2008. *See* PX 174 (May 22, 2008 check for $783,342.00 made payable to the

Treasurer of the United States); *see also* Jt. Stipl. I ¶ 29. On May 24, 2010, DCAA issued Revised Form 1, which superseded the Original Form 1 relating to SK 466 and CO 7 and disapproved $698,779.00 of KBR's incurred costs. *See* Jt. Stipl. I ¶¶ 26, 28. Although the Revised Form 1 questioned a lesser amount of plaintiff's costs, the difference between the two Form 1s—$84,563.00—has not yet been returned to KBR despite defendant's concession that plaintiff is entitled to its return. *See* Jt. Stipl. I ¶ 29; Def.'s Br. filed June 8, 2012, at 8 [No. 09–578C]. On December 19, 2008, plaintiff submitted a certified claim challenging the Government's withholding of the amount disapproved in the Original Form 1 regarding SK 466 and CO 7. Jt. Stipl. II ¶ 2. The claim was received by the cognizant Army contracting officer on December 23, 2008. *Id.*

Defendant's expert, Ms. Hadley, opined that DCAA was justified in challenging the prices at issue because KBR permitted ABC to bill in a manner other than that provided for in the contract. *See* DX 427, at 4. She testified that her review "started from scratch" and "compared each of the invoices that were submitted with the head band and the price that was identified in that invoice, compared it to the contract terms and identified those instances where the invoice had exceeded the contract terms for any of the price elements that were identified." Tr. at 1279 (Hadley). Having arrived at the same amount as DCAA, Ms. Hadley concluded that there were no errors in DCAA's review. *See* Tr. at 1279 (Hadley).

Ms. Hadley further testified that CO 7 "was an after the fact, sole source change order where the services provided by the subcontractor were a known item" and that she "didn't see any reason to actually create a fourth headband." Tr. at 1281 (Hadley). Because it applied retroactively, not only did CO 7 compensate ABC for the increased capacity, but it also "allowed [ABC] to bill at a headband that KBR knew that [ABC] hadn't reached at that point because head counts were already done and turned in." Tr. at 1281 (Hadley). Ms. Hadley expressed the opinion that the effect of CO 7 could have been accomplished by issuing a CO that provided for equitable reimbursement of the costs ABC incurred on account of the increased headcount. *See* Tr. at 1281 (Hadley). Mr. Check did not offer an opinion in No. 09–578C.

Procedural History

On July 2, 2009, plaintiff filed its complaint for breach of contract in No. 09–428C involving SK 465. KBR thereafter amended its complaint on August 3, 2009. The amendments were minor, non-substantive changes. On September 2, 2009, KBR filed its complaint for breach of contract in No. 09–578C involving SK 466. Although the parties agreed that these cases should not be consolidated, *see* Jt. Preliminary Status Report filed Oct. 22, 2009, at 1 [No. 09–428C]; Jt. Preliminary Status Report filed Dec. 22, 2009, at 1 [No. 09–578C], plaintiff moved to have these matters, as well as No. 10–839C, which KBR later sought to dismiss without prejudice, jointly tried, *see* Pl.'s Br. filed May 3, 2011, at 1 [Nos. 09–428C, –578C, 10–839C]. On May 23, 2011, the court granted KBR's unopposed motion to dismiss No. 10–839C without prejudice. On that same date, the court granted KBR's motion to have Nos. 09–428C and 09–578C jointly tried and entered an order setting trial to commence on December 12, 2011. *See* Order entered May 23, 2011 [Nos. 09–428C & –578C].

***32** On August 22, 2011, KBR filed a motion for partial summary judgment in No. 09–428C seeking judgment in its favor permitting it to recover its fixed base fee totaling $126,559.00. KBR argued that it would be entitled to its base fee whether or not its costs were deemed reasonable. *See* Pl.'s Br. filed Aug. 22, 2011, at 1. Defendant's responses to plaintiff's proposed findings of fact established that no genuine issue of material fact was present as to either the fixed nature of the base fee or the Army's obligation to pay KBR for completed performance under Task Orders 59 and 89. *See* Def.'s Resp. to Pl.'s Prop. Findings of Uncontr. Fact, Nos. 3, 4, 11, 18, 20, 22, 25, filed Sept. 22, 2011. Accordingly, the court determined that KBR was entitled to recover $84,789.00—the portion of its base fee not held by the Government as reserves; however, the court declined to enter judgment pending resolution of the balance of KBR's claims, concluding that the interests of justice and efficient judicial administration are not served by entry of a piecemeal judgment. *See* Order entered Oct. 25, 2011, at 2.

On November 11, 2011, KBR filed an unopposed motion for leave to present Ms. Battles's live testimony in January 2012 following the conclusion of the five-day trial scheduled to begin on December 12, 2011, because Ms. Battles was working as a civilian contractor for a company other than KBR in Iraq and was not available in December 2011. *See* Pl.'s Mot. filed Nov. 11, 2011, at 1–2 [No.

09–578C]. The court granted the unopposed motion on November 14, 2011. *See* Order entered Nov. 14, 2011 [Nos. 09–428C & –578C].

On November 29, 2011, defendant filed two motions *in limine*. The first, filed in both cases, sought to preclude testimony from Jennifer Freidenberg that is beyond her personal knowledge. The second, filed only in No. 09–578C, sought to exclude parol evidence concerning the SK 486 headband pricing. On that same date, KBR filed a motion *in limine* in both cases to exclude the testimony of defendant's expert witness, Ms. Hadley. By order entered December 8, 2011, the court denied defendant's motion to preclude testimony from Ms. Freidenberg, noting that plaintiff represented that Ms. Freidenberg would testify based on her personal knowledge and/or based on her personal knowledge of a review of plaintiff's books and records. *See* Order entered Dec. 8, 2011, at 2. Pursuant to that same order, the court granted in part and denied in part defendant's motion to exclude parol evidence in No. 09–578C. *See id.* The motion was granted insofar as plaintiff sought admission of parol evidence as to whether SK 466 required ABC to bill according to prices established for various headcount ranges. *See id.* The motion was denied to the extent plaintiff sought admission of documents that were created after execution of SK 466 and to the extent an exception to the parol evidence rule applied to specific documents or testimony offered. *See id.* The court also denied KBR's motion to exclude Ms. Hadley's testimony. *See id.*

Trial commenced on December 12, 2011, and proceeded through December 16, 2011, resuming on April 13, 2012, when Ms. Battles was available to testify. The parties presented their rebuttal cases on the next business day, April 16, 2012, and closing arguments were heard on April 17, 2012. Post-trial briefing was completed on June 29, 2012.

DISCUSSION

The Parties' Arguments

<u>No. 09–428C</u>

Plaintiff begins by explaining its relationship with its subcontractors in Iraq in 2004, noting that, although it had discretion to choose a subcontractor, KBR had no discretion to vary the subcontracted capacity from what the Army deemed was required regardless of the actual headcount at a particular site. *See* Pl.'s Br. filed May 25, 2012, at 18 [No. 09–428C]. Only the cognizant ACO possessed the authority to alter the stated capacity requirement through issuance of an LOTD. *See id.; see also* PX 6, at G–0202048. KBR was unable to account for this lack of discretion as it was forced to enter fixed-price—as opposed to cost-reimbursement—contracts with its subcontractors in Iraq because the subcontractors did not have Government-approved cost-accounting systems. ***33** *See* Pl.'s Br. filed May 25, 2012, at 18 [No. 09–428C]; Tr. at 832–33 (Check).

No. 09–428C involves SK 465, which KBR awarded to ABC on March 8, 2004, after receiving competitive proposals from six offerors. *See* Jt. Stipl. I ¶ 34; Pl.'s Br. filed May 25, 2012, at 20 [No. 09–428C]. Shortly thereafter, in June 2004, after having been instructed to cease performance at site H4, KBR was ordered to begin constructing a concrete DFAC facility and to prepare to serve an increased headcount of 6,200+ troops. *See* Pl.'s Br. filed May 25, 2012, at 21 [No. 09–428C]. KBR argues that "given the urgency of the LOTD, the fact that ABC was already in place and performing at Site H4 and the fact that KBR would have incurred significant demobilization and re-mobilization costs if it were to substitute a new subcontractor," it was reasonable to award the new work—to be memorialized in CO 1—to ABC without holding a competition. *Id.; see also* Tr. at 233–34, 337 (Donley). KBR was well-aware that time was of the essence because Major Hunter's June 7 LOTD had informed KBR that modifications to the existing contract were necessary "in the interest of force protection." JX 11.

Plaintiff further contends both that its decision not to hold a competition was reasonable and also that the prices in CO 1 themselves were reasonable. First, plaintiff notes that ABC's prices considered factors such as " 'existing site conditions and ... political conditions,' " including " 'the current violence and the beheading of hostages by terrorists [which] caused a drastic increase in the cost of labor and a severe shortage of available staff.' " Pl.'s Br. filed May 25, 2012, at 23 [No. 09–428C] (quoting PX 49). Despite this justification for the increase in ABC's CO 1 prices as compared to its prices for SK 465, "KBR did not simply accept ABC's June 27, 2004 proposal." *Id.* at 24. Rather, KBR sought additional information from ABC to assist in the evaluation of its proposal. *See id.;* PX 53. Mr. Al–Awadi provided KBR with equipment and staff lists, drawings and design layouts, and material schedules that were used in preparing ABC's CO 1 proposal. *See* PX 53. Although defendant faults KBR's records for failing to document that the increased violence in Iraq affected labor prices, Mr. Al–Awadi stated expressly when submitting the requested additional information that "the violence in Iraq lately has caused a severe shortage of staff that is willing to work in Iraq." *Id.* Mr. Donley's testimony confirmed this assessment. *See* Tr. at 323 (Donley) ("Because of this elevated amount of violence ... there was a very, very negative impact on the labor pool that was available."). Moreover, plaintiff explains that ABC was required to effect the changes detailed in the June 22 LOTD immediately-a difficult undertaking in that capacity was more than doubled and the concrete DFAC was an entirely different structure than the Kirby-style DFAC that was the subject of SK 465. *See* Pl.'s Br. filed May 25, 2012, at 21, 24 [No. 09–428C]; *see also* Tr. at 330 (Donley) ("There [was] an intense sense of urgency to get [the work specified in the June 22 LOTD] going. There was lots of pressure from the client [the Army] at the site. There was lots of pressure from the camp manager to begin this construction. The sooner it was built the sooner it would be offering the force protection that was requested by the client.").

Next, plaintiff relies on the fact that CO 1 was subject to KBR's greensheet-approval process, whereby various KBR personnel approved the prices proposed in CO 1 after conducting a price analysis. *See* Pl.'s Br. filed May 25, 2012, at 22–23 [No. 09–428C]. Contrary to defendant's accusations, plaintiff argues that its greensheet-approval process was not a rubber stamp of ABC's CO 1 proposal. KBR requested and received additional information from ABC before approving the proposed prices and then analyzed those prices in comparison to the SK 465 prices. *See id.* at 24–25. According to plaintiff, price analysis is a preferred method of determining reasonableness under the FAR, and KBR's price analysis—comparing the CO 1 prices to the SK 465 prices—was consistent with its established practices and allowed for a particularly accurate comparison because the SK 465 prices resulted from competition. *See id.* at 26. In performing its price analysis, KBR factored in the sudden modification of contractual requirements by the June 22 LOTD, increased violence, ***34** labor shortage, and sense of urgency that had not affected the prices in SK

465 and determined that the CO 1 prices were reasonable. *See id.* at 25, 28. Plaintiff admits that Mr. Nasery's PNM, which was a part of the CO 1 package reviewed during the greensheet-approval process, "could have better reflected the analytical bases for KBR's price reasonableness determination," *id.* at 27, but maintains that, given the "wartime circumstances," *id.*, its decision to incur the proposed costs was reasonable, even if the PNM "was not a model price analysis," *id.* at 28.

Plaintiff further notes that it provided Major Hunter with information and documentation regarding the cost increase from SK 465 to CO 1. *See id.* at 29; PX 63, at 1381. Major Hunter initially labored under the mistaken belief that ABC's cost for the concrete DFAC, exclusive of the DFAC services, was $33 million. *See* Pl.'s Br. filed May 25, 2012, at 30 [No. 09–428C]. He requested further clarification and information from Mr. Nasery in September 2004 and learned that "the $33 million amount that he mistakenly believed was for the facility *alone* was actually $37 million for both the facility and all of the other effort required to satisfy the capacity increase at Site H4 from 2573 to 6200 plus." *Id.; see also* PX 71. KBR also informed Major Hunter in September 2004 that the 6,200 headcount was "suspect," PX 71, at 4826, because the headcount had yet to exceed 2,500 troops. Pl.'s Br. filed May 25, 2012, at 31 [No. 09–428C]; PX 71, at 4826. Nonetheless, Major Hunter did not issue an LOTD altering the capacity requirement, so KBR and ABC continued to operate under an obligation to provide for a headcount of 6,200+. *See* Pl.'s Br. filed May 25, 2012, at 31 [No. 09–428C]. Plaintiff also argues that, although Major Hunter testified that he had a duty to object to costs or prices that he deemed unreasonable, *see* Tr. at 409–10 (Hunter), he never disagreed with the prices in CO 1. *See* Pl.'s Br. filed May 25, 2012, at 31 [No. 09–428C].

Plaintiff thus concludes, with respect to SK 465, that "in promptly requesting a proposal from ABC, probing the underpinnings of the proposed labor prices, performing both a technical and price analysis, and then executing CO 1 following receipt of required approvals [from the greensheet-approval process], KBR's DFAC Team personnel complied with KBR's established policies and procedures" in determining that the CO 1 prices were reasonable. *Id.* at 27. As further support, plaintiff proffers that its expert, Mr. Check, reached the same conclusion after comparing the CO 1 per-person prices at the SOW headcount (6,200+)

with the SK 465 per-person prices at the SOW headcount (2,573). *See id.* at 31–33. Mr. Check's analysis evaluated the price of the concrete DFAC separate from the other price components—labor, consumables, and kitchen equipment.[14] *See id.* at 32. Concluding that the price increase from SK 465 to CO 1 for labor, consumables, and kitchen equipment was 3.75%, Mr. Check opined that the CO 1 prices were reasonable, "particularly in light of the significant changes that were occurring in market and economic conditions at the time." *Id.* at 33. Mr. Check reached a similar conclusion after comparing the price of the H4 DFAC with the price of the D 16 DFAC. His analysis revealed that the D 16 DFAC, which had a lower SOW headcount than the H4 DFAC, was more expensive despite having less built-in force protection. *See id.* at 35. Consequently, plaintiff maintains that it has satisfied its burden of demonstrating that the CO 1 prices—including the price for the H4 DFAC—were reasonable.

Defendant takes the position that plaintiff is not entitled to recover any questioned amounts because KBR has failed to demonstrate, in accordance with FAR 31.201–3, that the costs incurred from ABC were reasonable. *See* Def.'s Br. filed June 8, 2012, at 4 [No. 09–428C]. FAR 31.201–3 provides that " '[a] cost is reasonable if, in its nature and amount, it does not exceed that which would be incurred by a prudent person in the ***35** conduct of competitive business.' "[15] *Id.* (quoting FAR 31.201–3(a)). Defendant advances the argument that, because plaintiff

---

[14] Mr. Check's analysis did not include reefers and generators because KBR maintains that the amounts for those items are not at issue in this case, as DCAA's Revised Form 1 did not question the amounts that KBR paid ABC for these items. *See* Pl.'s Br. filed May 25, 2012, at 3 [No. 09–578C].

[15] Defendant notes that the standard for reasonableness of costs "ha[s] not been of particular controversy in this litigation or in the litigation of the related case of *KBR I* [*see Kellogg Brown & Root Servs., Inc. v. United States,* 103 Fed.Cl. 714 (2012)] until KBR filed its post[-]trial brief here." Def.'s Br. filed June 8, 2012, at 5 [No. 09–428C]. In that brief plaintiff made "three bold new arguments with respect to the standard of review." *Id.* First, plaintiff alleged that, once it makes a *prima facie* showing of reasonableness, the burden of proof shifts to defendant to prove unreasonableness. *See id.* Next, plaintiff argued that the 1987 amendments improperly dispensed with the presumption of reasonableness and shifted the burden of proof to the contractor. *See id.* (citing Pl.'s Br. filed May 25, 2012, at 9 n. 6 [No. 09–428C]). Finally, plaintiff contended that the appropriate standard of review examines "whether the prices 'are caused by a contractor's gross disregard or willful misconduct by senior management with regard to contractual obligations.' " *Id.* (quoting Pl.'s Br. filed May 25, 2012, at 6 [No. 09–428C]). The court agrees with defendant that plaintiff's arguments are not supported by law and applies the standard as put forward by defendant. *See, e.g. supra* note 3.

failed to follow sound business practice particularly in its proper review of CO 1, it did not act as a reasonably prudent business. *See id.* at 8. In support of this argument, defendant highlights the flaws in Mr. Nasery's PNM and the greensheet-approval process that, arguably, did no more than rubberstamp an inadequate justification. *See id.* at 10–11. Defendant dismisses plaintiff's argument that the urgency of the situation led to the omissions and defects in Mr. Nasery's PNM because, as defendant explains, CO 1 was not signed until one month after it was requested. *See id.* at 9 n. 5. Moreover, although technical reviewers from KBR's Food Service Division commented that labor was "10 percent too expensive," *id.* at 9 (citing DX 103, at 0924), Mr. Nasery failed to address this concern with Mr. Al–Awadi; rather, "Mr. Nasery accepted [ABC's] first offer on the change order without any attempted revisions or 'push back,' " *id.* at 9–10.

In addition to his failure to engage in arm's-length negotiations with Mr. Al–Awadi, Mr. Nasery also relied on a flawed methodology in justifying the CO 1 prices in his PNM. *See id.* at 11. Defendant maintains that such a glaring flaw should have been discovered during the greensheet-approval process but was not because that process was merely "an uncritical 'rubber stamp' " of Mr. Nasery's justification. *Id.* Thus, defendant contends, KBR cannot argue that it employed sound business practices in deeming ABC's prices reasonable because "[e]ven the most cursory inspection of the total price of CO 1's newly [ ]proposed headbands, in comparison to those in the original SK 465, should [have] capture[d] the reviewer's attention, demonstrating a large jump, compared to the pre-existing cost trend." *Id.* at 12. Defendant supports its argument with Ms. Hadley's testimony, which revealed that the price increases for labor, equipment, reefers, generators, and consumables were out of proportion with the actual change in demand. *See id.* at 12–13; Tr. at 1241, 1249, 1251–53, 1259, 1261–62 (Hadley). As a final point underscoring the inadequacy of Mr. Nasery's PNM and the greensheet-approval process, defendant notes that the justification in the PNM was premised entirely on the fact that the SK 465 prices were the result of competition. *See* Def.'s Br. filed June 8, 2012, at 14 [No. 09–428C]. However, the award of SK 465 to ABC was the result of errors in the bad tabulation sheets. *See id.* Absent Mr. Nasery's errors in tabulating bids, ABC would not have been the lowest priced, technically acceptable bidder and may not have received the subcontract award. *See id.*

Defendant next addresses KBR's recognition of the inadequacy of the PNM in 2007 when it prepared two justifications for the costs of the concrete DFAC at site H4. *See id.* at 15. Defendant challenges the adequacy of the ICE because it compared the H4 DFAC to a facility located in Jordan—and thus subject to conditions far different from those in Iraq, which KBR contended greatly impacted costs—that was smaller in size and constructed two years after CO 1. *See id.* at 16–17. Moreover, KBR failed to offer a witness who could sponsor or explain the ICE: Mr. Castellana testified that he played no role in the creation of the ICE, Mr. Carr lacked knowledge regarding the facility used as a basis of comparison, and Mr. Check stated that he lacked the technical wherewithal***36** to analyze the ICE. *See id.;* Tr. at 474 (Castellana), 1721–22 (Check). Defendant further argues that the ICE was not a truly independent estimate because the individuals who prepared it knew the target price from the outset, thereby tainting the reliability of the analysis. *See* Def.'s Br. filed June 8, 2012, at 17 [No. 09–428C]; Tr. at 1221–22 (Hadley).

Mr. Castellana's 2007 Justification utilized the questionable ICE as a means for comparison, as well as the Kirby-style facility built at site D 16. *See* Def.'s Br. filed June 8, 2012, at 17–18 [No. 09–428C]. The H4 DFAC and D16 DFAC were constructed with different materials, using different methods, and at different times. *See id.* at 18. According to defendant, "[t]he only thing the two buildings had in common was a rough similarity in the number of people to be fed." *Id.* Although Mr. Castellana purported to provide a price justification based on a price comparison, the underlying comparables were either unpersuasive (the ICE) or inadequate (the dissimilar D16 DFAC). *See id.* at 18–19.

Defendant points out that even Mr. Check's expert price analysis does not demonstrate the reasonableness of the prices because it suffers from two flaws. Mr. Check concedes that what KBR purchased in SK 465 and CO 1 "was the right to give services to between 2501 soldiers and 3500 soldiers for a particular set price[.]" Tr. at 884 (Check); *see also* Def.'s Br. filed June 8, 2012, at 20 [No. 09–428C]. Accordingly, "[t]he SOW number plays no part in determining what KBR was obligated to pay ABC," Def.'s Br. filed June 8, 2012, at 20 [No. 09–428C], yet Mr. Check compared the per-person prices at the SOW figures in SK 465 and CO 1, not the stated price for the inclusive headcount band. Defendant argues that the comparison is meaningless because the SOW figures are "irrelevant (as to price)." *See id.* Indeed, Ms. Hadley re-performed Mr. Check's analysis by using the figures that represented the mid-point of the headcount bands in SK 465 and CO 1 that included the SOW numbers—instead of using the SOW figures, which fell at arbitrary points within the headcount band—and determined that there was "a far greater percentage increase in cost per person fed." *Id.*

The second flaw in Mr. Check's analysis, according to defendant, was his failure to consider items that KBR purchased via the two subcontracts. *See id.* at 19. He also did not factor in economies of scale that would have worked to ABC's benefit when it agreed to the capacity increase. *See id.* at 20–21. Defendant stresses that KBR's reliance on the increased violence in Iraq as contributing to higher labor prices is not supported by the record. *See id.* at 22. While defendant concedes that Iraq was a violent war zone during spring 2004, it questions the effect of the violence on labor prices, noting that "it was never used as a contemporaneous or near-contemporaneous explanation for the prices" and is particularly absent from the PNM, request for greensheet approval and KBR's internal documentation. *Id.* at 22–23. Noting that the third-country nationals who served as laborers did not know in advance to which site they would be assigned, defendant surmises that the spike in violence was not listed as the justification for the increased prices because it did not cause labor prices to rise. *See id.* at 23. Although Mr. Donley testified that he received phone calls from Mr. Al–Awadi expressing concern for his laborers' security, this testimony was undermined by the fact that, at the time Mr. Donley allegedly received these calls, no ABC employees were working at site H4; instead, the personnel at site H4 at that time were employees of a company that was working as ABC's labor subcontractor. *See id.* at 24–25.

Defendant makes the final point that, although the Revised Form 1 did not challenge reefers and generators specifically, it found KBR's justification of CO 1 completely flawed. *See id.* at 29. Consequently, defendant advocates, the court must determine a reasonable price for CO 1 because the record is devoid of evidence to support a finding by the court that even a portion of the CO 1 costs were reasonable, and, "in order for the Court to reconstruct CO 1 to determine a reasonable price, it must address all the price elements in that change order [including reefers and generators] in recognition of the

***37** fact that price negotiations may include trade-offs amongst price elements." *Id.* at 29–30.

No. 09–578C

Plaintiff challenges the Army's withholding payment by arguing that the Government misinterpreted KBR's contract with ABC when it contended that KBR was only obligated to pay ABC based on where the MAD headcount fell in a particular month. *See* Pl.'s Br. filed May 25, 2012, at 9 [No. 09–578C]. According to plaintiff, although "the consumables price ... would be paid within the headband where the maximum average daily headcount fell in a particular month[,]" the price paid for other items would be based on the SOW headcount. *Id.* at 10–11; *see also* Tr. at 109 (Carr). Mr. Carr testified as to the logic behind this type of payment scheme:

> BY MR. GALLAGHER:
>
> Q Other than consumables, you considered the [costs of] other[ ] [items] to be fixed?
>
> A Yes.
>
> Q Why was that?
>
> A The subcontractor was required to set up a facility to be prepared to serve the mid headband range. He had to put in place the reefers and the generators to service that facility, he had to bring the labor force on to serve that many people [specified in the SOW], so once he mobilized all that and put that in place, that was the level of effort that he was expending to perform that service and that's what entitled him to bill in the middle headband [i.e., the headband that encompassed the SOW headcount figure].

Tr. at 109–10 (Carr). As further evidence to undermine defendant's interpretation of SK 466 and CO 7, plaintiff draws the court's attention to ABC's invoices, which stated: "1. Cost of Operation is per SOW headcount range (2501–[3]500) including Labor since the contractual [*sic*] required number of Labor [*sic*] as per SOW is present on site. 2. Cost of consumables is per actual headcount range (1501–2500)." PX 185, at 6097; *see also* Pl.'s Br. filed May 25, 2012, at 15 [No. 09–578C].

Moreover, plaintiff contends that, when Mr. Carr created the new SK-type subcontract that utilized headcount bands, he discussed the structure with Army contracting personnel and explained that the upper and lower headcount bands were merely "prepriced options that could be utilized by KBR if and when the Government issued an LOTD or other required change to the Government directed capacity." Pl.'s Br. filed May 25, 2012, at 11 [No. 09–578C]. The Army personnel were pleased with the new subcontract structure and raised no objections. *See id.* at 11–12. Finally, plaintiff brands defendant's contention that KBR should have issued a lump-sum CO instead of creating a new headcount band to account for the troop surge at site H2 as "a last-ditch effort to try to re-write the terms" of SK 466 and CO 7. *See id.* at 16–17. Nonetheless, plaintiff rejoins that CO 7 essentially did what the Government contends KBR should have done in that CO 7 "made sure ABC was paid for the increased services ABC provided due to the surge in troops" in much the same way as a lump-sum CO providing for equitable reimbursement. *Id.* at 16–17.

Defendant responds that the terms of SK 466 and CO 7 are unambiguous and required KBR to pay ABC based on the actual monthly headcount. *See* Def.'s Br. filed June 8, 2012, at 5 [No. 09–578C]. Noting that Note 8 in SK 466 provides that " '[f]or other [non-SOW] headcount prices, refer to Tables 2, 3, and 4,' " *id.* at 6 (second alteration in original) (quoting PX 185, at 6454), defendant explains that Table 4 identifies only two variable price components—labor and consumables—indicating that all other price components are to be billed based on actual headcounts. *See id.* Defendant also interprets plaintiff's position as suggesting that the new headcount band added by CO 7 reflects a revised SOW headband and argues that such a position is implausible, given that CO 7 expressly states that " '[t]he Statement of Work remains unchanged.' " *See id.* at 8 (quoting JX 21, at G–0173882). According to defendant, plaintiff makes this argument

> because the premise of its contractual interpretation construct is that labor is always billed at the SOW rate[,] and it would be unable to recover the amounts overcharged***38**

> [i.e., amounts billed by ABC and paid by KBR for troops anticipated but not actually served] during the CO 7 period of performance if the additional headband in CO 7 were not considered to reflect the new SOW number.

Id. at 6–7. Despite plaintiff's attempt to characterize the new headcount band in such a way, defendant posits, the terms of CO 7 are consistent with defendant's construction of Table 4 that payment is to be based on actual headcounts. *See id.* at 7.

Defendant further questions KBR's decision to use a CO that required the creation of a new headcount band instead of issuing a lump-sum CO to reimburse ABC for the costs it incurred in preparing to feed the increased capacity. *See id.* at 7 n. 5. Ms. Hadley testified that

> [i]t would seem that you would just need to issue a change order to equitably reimburse the subcontractor for the increased costs ... but since [CO 7] was [issued] after the fact it allowed [ABC] to bill at a headband that KBR knew that [ABC] hadn't reached ... because head counts were already done and turned in.

Tr. at 1281 (Hadley). Despite the availability of this option, KBR did not consider it but now contends that its approach had the same effect and should be considered in a similar vein.

Standards for Cost Reasonableness

LOGCAP III incorporates FAR 52.216–7, which permits reimbursement of costs paid to ABC, the subcontractor, by plaintiff, the prime contractor, only to the extent that the contracting officer determines them to be allowable in accordance with FAR subpart 31.2. *See* FAR 52.216–7(a)(1) (2000)[16] ("The Government shall make payments to the Contractor ... in

[16] The court is unsure whether the parties are citing the current version of the FAR or the version that was in effect when LOGCAP III was awarded to KBR. Other than defendant's citation to FAR 52.216–7, *see* Def.'s Br. filed June 8, 2012, at 4 [No. 09–428C], the parties' citations to the FAR do not include dates. The court's review of the current and 2000 versions of the cited regulations revealed that, although minor formatting changes were made and a misplaced modifier was corrected, the regulations are almost identical. Accordingly, the version cited is inconsequential.

amounts determined to be allowable by the Contracting Officer in accordance with Subpart 31.2 of the Federal Acquisition Regulation (FAR)....”). Costs are allowable pursuant to FAR subpart 31.2 if they meet the standard for reasonableness. *See* FAR 31.201–2 (2000) (“The factors to be considered in determining whether a cost is allowable include the following: (1) Reasonableness.”). FAR 31.201–3 provides the standard for determining reasonableness, as follows:

(a) A cost is reasonable if, in its nature and amount, it does not exceed that which would be incurred by a prudent person in the conduct of competitive business. Reasonableness of specific costs must be examined with particular care in connection with firms or their separate divisions that may not be subject to effective competitive restraints. No presumption of reasonableness shall be attached to the incurrence of costs by a contractor. If an initial review of the facts results in a challenge of a specific cost by the contracting officer or the contracting officer’s representative, the burden of proof shall be upon the contractor to establish that such cost is reasonable.

(b) *What is reasonable depends upon a variety of considerations and circumstances,* including—

(1) Whether it is the type of cost generally recognized as ordinary and necessary for the conduct of the contractor’s business or the contract performance;
(2) Generally accepted sound business practices, arm’s length bargaining, and Federal and State laws and regulations;
(3) The contractor’s responsibilities to the Government, other customers, the owners of the business, employees, and the public at large; and
(4) Any significant deviations from the contractor’s established practices.

FAR 31.201–3 (2000) (emphasis added).

[1] Previously, a contractor’s incurred costs were entitled to a presumption of reasonableness, and the Government bore the ***39** burden of proving that the costs were unreasonable. *See Bruce Constr. Corp. v. United States,* 324 F.2d 516, 519 (Ct.Cl.1963). This presumption, however, was superseded in 1987 by an amendment to FAR 31.201–3. *See* 52 Fed.Reg. 19,800, 19,804

(May 27, 1987) (codified at FAR 31.201–3); *see Ace Constructors, Inc. v. United States,* 70 Fed.Cl. 253, 275 (2006); *George Sollitt Constr. Co. v. United States,* 64 Fed.Cl. 229, 245 (2005). The current version of FAR 31.201–3 squarely acknowledges the lack of that presumption and imposes on the contractor the burden of proof of reasonableness. *See* FAR 31.201–3(a) ("No presumption of reasonableness shall be attached to the incurrence of costs by a contractor.... [T]he burden of proof shall be upon the contractor to establish that such cost is reasonable."); *see also Lisbon Contractors, Inc. v. United States,* 828 F.2d 759, 767 (Fed.Cir.1987) ("The government was under no obligation to present evidence attacking an item if [the contractor] did not prove *prima facie* that it was properly included."); *Thermalon Indus., Ltd. v. United States,* 51 Fed.Cl. 464, 472 (2002); *McDonnell Douglas Corp. v. United States,* 40 Fed.Cl. 529, 536 (1998), *rev'd on other grounds,* 182 F.3d 1319 (Fed.Cir.1999); *Fiber Materials, Inc.,* ASBCA No. 53616, 07–1 BCA ¶ 33,563, 2007 WL 1252481 (Apr. 17, 2007). Thus, the court holds that plaintiff's burden was to prove by a preponderance of evidence the reasonableness of its claimed costs.

FAR 31.201–3 affords the court significant discretion in determining whether claimed costs are reasonable and sets forth a non-exhaustive list of circumstances to be considered. *See* FAR 31.201–3(b)(1)–(4). Despite this guidance, case law in which a court or the Armed Services Board of Contract Appeals (the "ASBCA") has exercised its discretion and evaluated the reasonableness of a claimed cost in similar circumstances is limited.[17] Plaintiff relies on *Lockheed Martin Tactical Aircraft Systems,* ASBCA No. 49530, 00–1 BCA ¶ 30,852, 2000 WL 307741 (Mar. 22, 2000), to support its argument that its costs were reasonable. *See* Pl.'s Br. filed May 25, 2012, at 16, 33–34 [No. 09–428C]. *Lockheed* involved the production and sale of military aircraft for the Government of Turkey through the Department of Defense's Foreign Military Sales program (the

[17] Most of the cases addressing the reasonableness of claimed costs involve challenges to the amount of employee compensation. *See Sterling Millwrights, Inc. v. United States,* 26 Cl.Ct. 49, 97–98 (1992) (citing FAR 31.201–3(b) and stating that "the reasonableness of compensation is a question of fact that is determined in light of all the relevant facts of a particular case" (citations omitted)); *Boeing Aerospace Operations, Inc.,* ASBCA Nos. 46274, 46275, 94–2 BCA ¶ 26,802, 1994 WL 96970 (Mar. 21, 1994) (determining reasonableness of employee compensation by considering "all of the relevant circumstances existing at the time of the incurrence of the costs" (citation omitted)), *aff'd on recons.,* ASBCA Nos. 46274, 46275, 94–3 BCA ¶ 27,281, 1994 WL 651887 (Nov. 9, 1994).

"FMSP"). *Lockheed,* 00–1 BCA ¶ 30,852, at 152,294. Pursuant to the FMSP, the United States enters an agreement with a foreign country—the customer—to serve as the customer's agent and contracts with a United States contractor for the production of specified goods. *Id.* The United States, as an agent for Turkey, contracted with Lockheed for the production of military aircraft. *Id.* at 152,296–97. In conjunction with Turkey's purchase through the FMSP, the United States brokered a counter-trade military agreement between the Governments of Egypt and Turkey whereby co-production of the aircraft would be performed by a subcontractor in Egypt. *Id.* The United States was aware that Turkey would incur significant co-production premiums on account of this arrangement. *Id.* at 152,312.

When Lockheed sought reimbursement of costs incurred in connection with co-production efforts, the United States, contending that the costs were unreasonable, disallowed them. *Id.* The ASBCA disagreed. *Id.* at 152,313. Explaining that FAR 31.201–3 provides for an evaluation of reasonableness on the basis of the specific circumstances presented, the ASBCA discussed the "unique facts at work ... specifically, the period of political and military turmoil which formed the backdrop of th[e] case." *Id.* at 152,312–13. The ASBCA recognized that such circumstances will alter the costs of services and stated that "[u]nusually high costs may be necessary where urgency is present or where no alternative sources are available." ***40** *Id.* at 152,312 (citation omitted) (internal quotation marks omitted). Moreover, the ASBCA noted that the United States, aware of the high estimate for the co-production premium, encouraged Turkey to proceed with the contract, thereby implying that the co-production costs were reasonable. *See id.* at 152,312–13. When it later disallowed those costs, the United States failed to explain why costs previously deemed reasonable had since become unreasonable. *Id.* at 152,312. Accordingly, the ASBCA ruled that Lockheed reasonably incurred the total amount of co-production costs claimed and was entitled to recover them in full. *See id.* at 152,313.

Although the ASBCA acknowledged that Lockheed's claimed co-production costs were significant, it recognized that production was occurring in the midst of "political and military turmoil," likely resulting in elevated prices for services rendered. *Id.* at 152,312. Plaintiff thus urges that, in evaluating the reasonableness of its claimed subcontractor costs, the court should consider the wartime environment in which KBR was operating. *See* Pl.'s Br. filed May 25, 2012, at 33–34 [No. 09–428C].

While the court considers the violence in Iraq as a circumstance bearing on the reasonableness of the agreed-upon prices, the court emphasizes that the determination is not what the court considers to be reasonable; rather, the court will examine whether plaintiff's evidence supports the claimed amounts as reasonable. In *KBR I* this court had a benchmark against which to evaluate the questioned amounts. *See* 103 Fed.Cl. at 769–70. DCAA in that case had questioned the reasonableness of some of the prices that KBR paid for services performed by its subcontractor and then passed on to the Government as reimbursable costs. The court compared those prices to the prices proposed by the subcontractor in its subsequent competitive bid submitted to the Army in an attempt to win a fixed-price contract for the same services that had been performed by KBR as the prime contractor. *See id.* In concluding that the some of the prices paid were reasonable, the court explained that the "reasonableness of a price can only be judged in terms of some other price figure[,] [and] [i]t is from this other figure, the conceptual anchor point, that one determines if the questioned price is reasonable." *Id.* at 769. It is from this perspective that the court undertakes to determine whether the questioned costs in these matters are reasonable.

No. 09–428C

[2] This case took an interesting turn when plaintiff filed its opening post-trial brief, which revealed that plaintiff was adding a new dimension to the position that it had taken before and during trial regarding the standard of review for determining the reasonableness of costs. Throughout trial the standard for determining the reasonableness of costs—set forth above—did not appear to be in dispute; yet, in its post-trial brief, plaintiff advanced a new position, arguing that, in a cost-reimbursement contract, "a contractor's costs are allowable ... unless they are caused by a contractor's gross disregard or willful misconduct by senior management with regard to its contractual obligations." Pl.'s Br. filed May 25, 2012, at 6 [No. 09–428C]; *see also supra* note 15.

Plaintiff contends that it has established a *prima facie* case demonstrating that the costs at issue fit within this standard for reasonableness. *See* Pl.'s Br. filed May 25, 2012, at 3 [No. 09–428C]. Plaintiff argues that it satisfied its burden by showing that (1) it incurred the questioned costs in connection with its performance of TO 59, (2) the prices in CO 1 were the result of its best efforts to perform under TO 59 in wartime circumstances, and (3) the incurred costs were not the product of management's gross disregard or willful misconduct. *See id.* at 7; *see also* Pl.'s Br. filed June 22, 2012, at 5 [No. 09–428C]. Because of this showing, plaintiff maintains, the burden shifted to defendant to show that the costs were unreasonable.[18]

***41** Defendant balks at plaintiff's characterization of the standard for determining the reasonableness of the costs in CO 1, and objects that plaintiff is only now—post-trial—raising this argument. Despite plaintiff's assertion that, "[i]n substance, the Government is attempting to fundamentally alter more than 50 years of established practice regarding cost reasonableness under cost reimbursement contracts[,]" Pl.'s Br. filed June 22, 2012, at 3 [No. 09–428C], defendant argues that it is "apply[ing] the law as-written and contained in the FAR[,]" Def.'s Br. filed June 29, 2012, at 4 [No. 09–428C]. Defendant thus contends that the standard of review in this case—as set forth above—utilizes the "prudent businessperson" standard set forth in FAR 31.201–3. *See id.* The court agrees, recognizing that in various cases since passage of the 1987 FAR amendments the Federal Circuit and the Court of Federal Claims have applied the post-amendment version of FAR 31.201–3 without restricting its application to indirect costs. *See supra* at 38–39. Furthermore, the court finds it likely that, had plaintiff raised this argument before or during trial,

[18] Plaintiff admits that it bears the burden of proof as to questioned indirect costs, yet makes the argument that the 1987 amendments to the FAR improperly assigned the burden of proof to the contractor with respect to incurred direct costs by dispensing with the presumption of reasonableness that previously applied to costs incurred by a contractor. *See* Pl.'s Br. filed May 25, 2012, at 9 n. 6 [No. 09–428C]. Despite the fact that the language of FAR 31.201–3 does not limit itself to indirect costs, as defendant has noted, *see* Def.'s Br. filed June 29, 2012, at 4 n. 1 [No. 09–428C], plaintiff asserts that "there is ample support for the Court to continue to apply the presumption that KBR's incurred direct costs are reasonable," *see* Pl.'s Br. filed May 25, 2012, at 9 n. 6 [No. 09–428C], and urges the court to apply the presumption to its direct costs, notwithstanding its argument that it made a *prima facie* showing that satisfied its burden, *id.* at 7. The court declines plaintiff's request because FAR 31.201–3 expressly dispenses with the presumption of reasonableness and applies to "costs" without restricting its application to indirect costs. *See* FAR 31.201–3 (2012).

defendant would have presented its case differently and questioned KBR's former and current personnel in a different vein.[19]

The court finds that KBR has not shown that it employed sound business practices and acted as a reasonably prudent business in accepting ABC's proposed prices for CO 1. The court accepts KBR's decision not to hold a competition upon receiving the June 22 LOTD as reasonable, given the sense of urgency conveyed by Major Hunter and the Army. That urgency, however, is insufficient to justify the acceptance of unreasonable prices. Moreover, while it does appear that KBR—whether pursuant to its request or not—received additional information from ABC supporting the prices in the latter's proposal, this, too, is insufficient to establish reasonableness. This information did not illuminate the costs of the components that ABC would provide; rather, the documents that Mr. Al–Awadi submitted to Mr. Nasery in July 2004 merely identified the numbers of each component that would be provided, the number of laborers for each job title that would be necessary, the layout of the new DFAC, and a schedule of materials to be used. *See* PX 53.

Plaintiff emphasizes the particularly exigent circumstances, dangerous wartime conditions, and need immediately to increase capacity, taking issue with defendant's and DCAA's after-the-fact challenges to KBR's decisions

[19] Notwithstanding the foregoing, if plaintiff's argument that costs are presumed reasonable unless they resulted from management's gross disregard or willful misconduct had merit, plaintiff almost certainly has not demonstrated reasonableness. The problem is that KBR's witnesses and documents admit that plaintiff was aware that the PNM was inadequate. *See* Tr. at 172–73 (Carr), 366–68 (Donley), 485–86 (Castellana); DX 90, at 3770, 3783. While Mr. Nasery's failure to investigate the Food Service Division's concern that labor was too expensive may not have been readily apparent to the four KBR employees (Messrs. Donley, Parenti, Agness, and Quigley) involved in the greensheet-approval process, surely the significant price increase from SK 465 to CO 1 would have raised a red flag, leading the reviewers to discover Mr. Nasery's flawed methodology that compared SK 465 prices with the CO 1 prices on the basis of a doubled quantity and a doubled rate. *See* Tr. at 334 (Donley) (stating that greensheet-approval process would have included thorough review of PNM). Alas, Messrs. Donley and Quigley approved CO 1 without detecting the analytical flaw, reducing greensheet approval to little more than a rubber stamp. Having failed to detect what appears to be a glaring miscalculation after an admittedly "thorough[ ] review[ ][of] all the required [CO 1] documents," Tr. at 332 (Donley), KBR's management acted with gross disregard for the reasonableness of the proposed prices and cannot satisfy the standard advanced by plaintiff.

made in such an environment. ***42** Plaintiff responds to defendant's contention that KBR never documented the effect of these conditions on the labor market by citing Mr. Al–Awadi's e-mails to Mr. Nasery in June and July 2004, *see* PX 49; PX 53, as well as Mr. Donley's testimony that he "received daily phone calls" from Mr. Al–Awadi expressing concern for the safety of his laborers, Tr. at 214 (Donley). The court finds that, while Mr. Al–Awadi did mention the effect of the violence on labor prices in his e-mails to Mr. Nasery, his statements appear to be self-serving, given that neither Mr. Nasery nor anyone else in KBR's employ ever cited this as a justification for the dramatic price increase in CO 1.

Furthermore, KBR never sought information from ABC as to how the violence-induced price increase for labor manifested. In a July 2004 e-mail to Mr. Nasery, Mr. Al–Awadi remarked that the "increased cost of labor ... includes salaries, benefits, indemnity, bonuses, medical examinations, insurance, [and] air tickets from home countries to Kuwait." PX 53. He also attributed increased labor costs to the need to fly laborers to Turkey or Jordan from Kuwait and then transport them by road to the sites in Iraq. *See id.* While Mr. Al–Awadi's explanation is logical, KBR accepted it at face value, never seeking further explanation assigning some dollar value to the cost elements. In light of the significant increase, it was unreasonable for KBR to accept this overview of the situation because KBR knew that its subcontractors did not maintain documentary support and would not be able to provide support for the increased costs if the issue were not pressed with Mr. Al–Awadi in this time frame. As for Mr. Al–Awadi's daily phone calls to Mr. Donley, no ABC employees were working at site H4 at the time these calls allegedly took place. Although the court does not doubt that site H4 experienced a dramatic spike in violence around June 2004, the court has no confidence in plaintiff's assertion that this resulted in an increase in labor costs commensurate with that from SK 465 to CO 1. *Compare* JX 10, at 83026, *with* PX 58, at 0609.

One recurrent point of disagreement between the parties was whether KBR—and, consequently, ABC—was responsible for its laborers being on or off site in accordance with capacity fluctuations. The court finds defendant's position unreasonable that KBR and ABC were required to send laborers offsite when the headcount dipped below that specified in the SOW, only to recall them when capacity increased. Although keeping unnecessary laborers onsite resulted in the Army at times paying for manpower that it did not require, KBR's decision avoided the Army's incurring excessive mobilization and demobilization costs. It is from this refined perspective that the court considers Mr. Check's testimony supporting the reasonableness of the pricing and Ms. Hadley's criticism of it. *See* Tr. at 1265–69 (Hadley); DX 105, at 7.

Despite the fact that SK 465 was executed only four months before CO 1, *compare* JX 10, with PX 58, some level of price increase is warranted due to the admitted fast-track order to provide for greater capacity. Nonetheless, Mr. Check's premise—which compared the prices in SK 465 and CO 1 based on the SOW targets (2,573 and 6,200+, respectively) that fell toward the high end of the headcount band in CO 1 (5,501–6,500) and the low end of the headcount band in SK 465 (2,501–3,500)—is unreasonable. *See* PX 142, at 11. This methodology had the effect of basing a comparison on per-person prices that were meaningless in that they did not measure the same thing. In other words, the per-person price for 6,200 troops represented the price per person when ABC was serving almost the highest number of troops falling within a given headcount band; consequently, the per-person price will be lower than when ABC is serving a capacity that falls toward the lower end of the headcount band, as is the case with Mr. Check's per-person price for the SK 465 SOW target. Such a comparison is neither meaningful nor useful in determining the price increase from SK 465 to CO 1 because it fails to measure the overall price increase and, instead, measures the per-person price increase at different activity levels. *See id.; see also* Tr. at 1273 (Hadley) ("In the beginning of the headband the contractor is earning much more price per person, a much higher profit than it would be when they're serving at the high ***43** end of the band because they obviously have to provide more services [when providing at the high end of the band].").

Ms. Hadley's analysis revealed the above defect inherent in Mr. Check's approach. *See* DX 106, at 1 (Ms. Hadley's demonstrative exhibit rebutting Mr. Check's analysis); Tr. at 1274–75 (Hadley) ("[Y]ou can't compare the price from the beginning of the headband to the price in another head band at the high end of the headband because you're providing a different level of productivity and a different level of service."). To demonstrate her point, Ms. Hadley re-worked Mr. Check's analysis using the mid-point of the headcount bands that encompassed the SOW targets. *See* DX 106, at 2. Although Ms. Hadley did not identify the percentage increase yielded by her analysis, she depicted a much steeper price increase than that depicted by Mr. Check. *See id.* Moreover, as evidenced by Ms. Hadley's graphic depiction of monthly prices by element reproduced on page 19, monthly prices for individual elements doubled or more than doubled from SK 465 to CO 1. *See* DX 91, at 11. This casts serious doubt on Mr. Check's report of a 3.75% price increase.

Ms. Hadley did not offer her own assessment of damages, nor was she required to do so. Urging that the court accept her determination that the results of Mr. Check's analysis are "badly skewed," *see* Def.'s Br. filed June 29, 2012, at 12, defendant correctly observes that

> the SOW numbers defined nothing in terms of KBR's contractual obligations to ABC (which is what is relevant in evaluating the reasonableness of the contract between KBR and ABC)[;] regardless of where on a headband the number of troops fed fell, ABC was entitled to the exact same amount of money.

Id. The 3.75% price increase—which could appear to be a modest increase, given the level of violence and urgency of the situation—advanced by Mr. Check is not representative of the actual price increase from SK 465 to CO 1. The court lacks a reliable contemporaneous benchmark against which to assess the CO 1 prices to determine if they are in fact reasonable. Accordingly, the court finds that plaintiff has failed to demonstrate the reasonableness of the costs incurred for pricing elements—not including facility costs—that were questioned by DCAA in its Revised Form 1.[20]

Ms. Hadley did prepare a demonstrative exhibit that forms the basis for a reasonable price for CO 1 based on SK 465's per-item prices for dining

[20] The court recognizes the Revised Form 1 as the operative document questioning KBR's incurred costs. Consequently, the court has not accepted defendant's challenge to KBR's costs incurred for reefers and generators because those items were not questioned by DCAA in the Revised Form 1. *See* JX 36. To the extent the Government is withholding from KBR monies it is owed for reefers and generators, KBR is entitled to return of those amounts.

equipment, labor, and generators and the prices per headcount average, e.g., 4,000 would be the headcount average for the 3,501–4,500 headcount band) for consumables and reefers. *See* DX 105. Ms. Hadley applied these essentially unit prices to the corresponding headcount average and number of required items in CO 1. Ms. Hadley then concluded that the CO 1 prices that devolved from the SK 465 prices represented what would have been a reasonable price for CO 1. The total for Mr. Hadley's estimated CO 1 was $20,821,188.00 or $1,735,099.00 per month, as compared to CO 1's actual total and monthly costs of $31,308,000.00 and $2,609,000.00, respectively.[21] Ms. Hadley next determined the total difference between the actual CO 1 price and her estimated reasonable price—a total of $9,304,181.00.[22] ***44** Plaintiff argues that, because Ms. Hadley, as defendant's expert, abandoned the $12.5–million amount questioned by DCAA in its Revised Form 1 in favor of her calculation, *see* Tr. at 1549–50 (Hadley), defendant should no longer be heard to argue in support of the $12.5–million amount, *see* Pl.'s Br. filed May 25, 2012, at 37 [No. 09–428C]. The result of Ms. Hadley's analysis—as corrected by the court's calculations and reduced by the amounts listed for reefers and generators, which the court has determined are not at issue—represents the new total of questioned costs. Accordingly, the total amount of questioned costs becomes $8,300,292.00, i.e., $10,486,812.00–$2,186,520.00 (Ms. Hadley's questioned amount for reefers and generators) = $8,300,292.00. Thus, KBR is entitled to $4,229,212.00, i.e., the difference between Ms. Hadley's questioned amount, which represents reasonable adjustments that plaintiff cannot overcome, less reefers and generators and the $12,529,504.00 questioned in the Revised Form 1.

---

[21] The total and monthly costs for CO 1, as executed, are derived from the monthly prices listed in the "Pricing" section of CO 1, as well as ABC's proposal. *See* PX 58, at 0609. A discrepancy is apparent between the total cost of CO 1, as noted by the parties, which at times was $33 million and at other times was $37 million, and the total derived from the court's calculation. The cause of the discrepancy is unclear, and for purposes of this exercise, the court will adopt its own calculation based on the figures in CO 1 offered as an exhibit at trial.

[22] By the court's calculation, the actual difference is $10,486,812.00. Ms. Hadley testified that to arrive at the $9.3–million amount, she first calculated the difference between the actual CO 1 monthly price and the estimated CO 1 monthly price ($2,609,000.00—$1,735,099.00 = $873,901.00) and then multiplied the difference by twelve to arrive at the total difference for the year ($873,901.00 x 12 = $10,486,812.00). *See* Tr. at 1266–67 (Hadley). Utilizing this same analysis, the court arrived at $10,486,812.00, not the $9,304,181.00 obtained by Ms. Hadley. The court will use the $10–million figure, which is the correct result of Ms. Hadley's equation.

As a final point, plaintiff made the observation at trial that Ms. Hadley's analysis inexplicably used the lowest headcount band when determining CO 1 and estimated CO 1 prices instead of using the middle headcount band that contained the SOW target. *See* Tr. at 1688–89 (Check). Moreover, she calculated the price per headcount average using the highest band in SK 465. *See* DX 105. It is unclear why Ms. Hadley opted to use these headcount bands, although it appears that she was attempting to depict what would have been a natural progressive increase from one band to the next, i.e., from the 3,501–4,500 headcount band in SK 465 to the 4,501–5,500 headcount band in CO 1. The court notes, however, that the difference between the proposed prices for the low and middle headcount bands in actual CO 1 was *de minimis*. *See* PX 58, at 0609 (chart indicates that only the price for consumables differs from the low headcount band to the middle headcount band). Ms. Hadley's result would not have differed significantly had she carried her analysis through to the middle headcount band.

The court emphasizes that the burden was not defendant's to prove the reasonableness of KBR's claimed costs. The court found Ms. Hadley's approach, with the court's modifications discussed above, adduced the more reliable method for assessing the reasonableness of the increased prices from the benchmark SK 465 prices. The court sees no need for a further adjustment due to its rejection of Ms. Hadley's consideration to economies of scale. The court must be conservative in making allowances in plaintiff's favor after finding KBR's direct evidence and documents less persuasive on labor costs.

KBR's incurred facility costs were considered separately by Ms. Hadley and Mr. Check. One initial dispute that was resolved during trial was the location of the Q–West facility used for comparison in the ICE. It ultimately was determined that that facility was located in Jordan—not Iraq. *See* Def.'s Br. filed June 8, 2012, at 16–17 [No. 09–428C]. Neither expert relied on Mr. Nasery's PNM, and Ms. Hadley denounced it as flawed. *See* DX 91, at 11, 23; Tr. at 1642, 1644–45, 1648 (Check). In analyzing the building price, Mr. Check reviewed Mr. Castellana's 2007 Justification, which KBR admittedly had prepared at a significant remove. Similar to the 2007 Justification, Mr. Check compared the DFAC at site H4 to the DFAC at site D16 because the SOW targets for each DFAC were relatively close. *See* PX 142, at 10. After factoring in an estimated cost to provide external force protection to the D 16 facility, Mr. Check determined a price per person for each facility. Because the per-person price for the H4 facility was lower, Mr. Check concluded that the price of the H4 DFAC was reasonable, especially because the H4 DFAC had even greater force protection—which would have increased the cost—than that factored in to the price of the D16 facility. *See* Tr. at 830 (Check).

Ms. Hadley's analysis of the building price began with an error. In comparing the price ***45** of the H4 facility to that of the Q–West facility used for comparison in the ICE, Ms. Hadley deducted the Iraq adjustment that had been added to the cost of the D 16 facility to account for the fact that it was constructed outside of Iraq in a region subject to different conditions. *See* DX 105, at 6. Because it has been determined that Q–West was located outside Iraq, the Iraq adjustment should not have been deducted from the cost of that facility. *See* Tr. at 1227–28 (Hadley) (stating assumption Iraq adjustment was figure added to facility built outside of Iraq when that facility is being compared to facility within Iraq). After deducting the Iraq adjustment, Ms. Hadley determined a monthly cost for both the Q–West and H4 facilities. *See* DX 105, at 6. Performing this same analysis without deducting the Iraq adjustment yields a monthly cost of $565,102.00 for the Q–West building, i.e., $6,781,224.00 ÷ 12 months. The monthly cost for the H4 DFAC was $566,000.00. *See id.* Thus, the H4 DFAC is only slightly more expensive than the Q–West facility, which was approximately 500 square meters smaller even after the addition of a square-footage adjustment to its cost. *See* DX 90, at 3783; Tr. at 182–83 (Carr). Tellingly, Ms. Hadley opined that "the size of the building and the type of construction have a much more significant impact on the reasonableness of the price than a head count capacity would." Tr. at 1217 (Hadley). If this is so, then the cost of the H4 DFAC appears even more reasonable, given that it is so close in cost to the Q–West facility that, although constructed of concrete, was smaller and lacked the bells and whistles included in the H4 building. *See* PX 51, at 1400; PX 84, at 0562.

The court recognizes that KBR's justification for its facility costs (the 2007 Justification) was prepared long after KBR had agreed to the prices proposed by ABC in CO 1. Nonetheless, given the increased capacity, sudden change in type of construction, and evidence that various VIP extras were required, the court finds that the costs KBR incurred for the construction of the H4 DFAC are reasonable. As the experts' analyses have revealed, the cost of the H4 DFAC was not significantly greater than either of the two facilities used as comparables, despite the fact that it was a larger, better protected structure whose construction resulted from an urgent LOTD that vastly altered the previous requirements. Accordingly, the court finds that KBR is entitled to payment of the amounts questioned by DCAA relating to the facility lease.

No. 09–578C

[3] Defendant's challenge in this case is one of contract interpretation. According to defendant, KBR was only obligated to pay ABC based on where the MAD headcount fell in a particular month, contrary to KBR's assertion that, for all items except consumables, it was obligated to pay ABC based on the SOW figure regardless of actual headcount levels. *See* Def.'s Br. filed June 8, 2012, at 5–6 [No. 09–578C]. KBR explains that the two headcount bands in addition to the middle headcount band, i.e., the SOW band, were merely pre-priced options that could be utilized by the Army if it issued a LOTD changing the required capacity. The parties' positions pit testimony from two KBR employees against each other. Defendant relies on testimony from Ms. Battles who stated that CO 7 did not provide explicitly for payment to ABC pursuant to the new (and highest) headcount band regardless of the actual headcount. *See* Tr. at 1611 (Battles). Mr. Carr, on the other hand, testified that, because ABC set up its facility to accommodate the capacity specified in the SOW and prepared to serve that number of troops, it was entitled to be paid in accordance with the SOW target without reference to actual headcounts. *See* Tr. at 109–10 (Carr).

By creating a new headcount band in CO 7 to provide a pricing structure for the troop surge, defendant contends that KBR was creating a new SOW band, given that its position previously had been that payment was to be made in accordance with the SOW capacity figure. *See* Def.'s Br. filed June 8, 2012, at 6 [No. 09–578C]. This, defendant argues, is implausible because CO 7 clearly stated that the SOW was unchanged from that in SK 466. *See id.* at 6–8. Plaintiff responds that, once ABC incurred costs to serve the capacity set forth in the SOW, it ***46** was entitled to be paid for those services even if actual headcounts dipped below the SOW figure because preparations already had been made and ABC was not able to reduce its labor pool or return kitchen equipment with every incidental change in capacity. *See* Pl.'s Br. filed May 25, 2012, at 13 [No. 09–578C]. However, once capacity increased on account of the troop surge in January 2005, a new pricing structure was necessary to ensure payment to ABC for costs incurred in preparing to serve the influx.

Plaintiff also asks the court to adopt its resolution with ABC of how to charge for serving a capacity level that exceeded that provided for in the highest headcount band. Defendant counters that, rather than addressing the issue unilaterally by creating a new headcount band, KBR should have issued a lump-sum CO or required ABC to submit a request for equitable adjustment to obtain reimbursement of the excess costs it incurred. *See* Def.'s Br. filed June 29, 2012, at 8–9 [No. 09–578C]; Def.'s Br. filed June 8, 2012, at 7 n. 5 [No. 09–578C]; Tr. at 1281 (Hadley).

Although the parties disagree as to SK 466's and CO 7's payment terms, it is undeniable that, for some time in 2005, headcounts at site H2 exceeded what was provided for in SK 466's pre-priced headcount bands. Some construct was necessary to deal with wartime exigencies that resulted in this rapidly increased capacity. If a new construct had not been established, ABC would be faced with the draconian choice of feeding the influx of troops and risking nonpayment for costs incurred in serving a capacity not provided for in the existing headcount band structure or feeding only the maximum number of troops provided for in the existing bands. While defendant may have a point that a lump-sum CO or request for equitable adjustment may have been equally effective in compensating ABC for its incurred costs, KBR's approach of creating a new headcount band was reasonable in the circumstances. The prices in the new band were derived by computing an incremental increase from the prices in the existing headcount bands that were established competitively. The court thus has an appropriate benchmark against which to measure the reasonableness of the prices in the new band. Consequently, despite the availability of other options for reimbursing ABC, the court finds that KBR acted reasonably when faced with a sudden increase in capacity in this wartime environment and is entitled to reimbursement of costs paid to ABC in the amount questioned in the Revised Form 1 (plus $84,563.00, which represents the difference between the amounts questioned in the Original and Revised Form 1s that has not yet been returned to KBR).

CONCLUSION

Accordingly, based on the foregoing,

1. By October 19, 2012, the parties shall submit a Joint Stipulation,[23] consistent with the directions listed below, reflecting the amount of judgment to be entered in each case for plaintiff:

    (a) To the extent that KBR remitted payment to DCAA for reefers and generators following DCAA's issuance of its Original Form 1 regarding SK 465 and CO 1, KBR is entitled to return of that amount because those items were not questioned in the Revised Form 1 for SK 465 and CO 1 and therefore have not been put in issue.

    (b) In accordance with the order entered October 25, 2011, on Plaintiff's Motion for Partial Summary Judgment on Liability, plaintiff is entitled to its base fee in the amount of $84,789.00, which represents the portion of its base fee not held as reserves.

    (c) An award of $4,229,212.00 for reasonable costs, which represents the difference between Ms. Hadley's questioned amounts in SK 465 and CO 1 and the amounts questioned by DCAA in the Revised Form 1. This amount shall be adjusted for applicable contract additions.

    (d) The amount of facility lease costs relating to SK 465 and CO 1 that were withheld from KBR.

    (e) The total amount questioned in the Revised Form 1 regarding SK 466 and CO ***47** 7, i.e., $698,779.00, and challenged by KBR, plus $84,563.00, which represents the difference between the amounts questioned in the Original Form 1 and the Revised Form 1 that KBR remitted to DCAA but that has not yet been returned to KBR despite defendant's concession that plaintiff is entitled to the latter.

[23] Agreement to the amounts signifies that they represent only the amounts awarded to plaintiff in both actions, but does not signify that either party concurs in the awards.

2. When the court orders entry of judgment, the Clerk of the Court will be directed to enter judgment for plaintiff consistent with the total of the amounts reflected in the parties' Joint Stipulation, including interest pursuant to 41 U.S.C. § 7109 (2006), from October 6, 2008, for KBR's claim related to SK 465 and CO 1, and from December 23, 2008, for KBR's claim related to SK 466 and CO 7. Each party shall bear its own costs.

IT IS SO ORDERED.

Fed.Cl.,2012.

Kellogg Brown & Root Services, Inc. v. U.S.

107 Fed.Cl. 16

END OF DOCUMENT

ASPATORE